Intimate Partner Violence in the Black Church

Intimate Partner Violence in the Black Church

Bridging the Gap between Awareness and Policy Development

Carlos Jermaine Richard

WIPF & STOCK · Eugene, Oregon

INTIMATE PARTNER VIOLENCE IN THE BLACK CHURCH
Bridging the Gapbetween Awareness and Policy Development

Copyright © 2017 Carlos Jermaine Richard. All rights reserved. Except for brief quotations in critical publications or reviews, no part of this book may be reproduced in any manner without prior written permission from the publisher. Write: Permissions, Wipf and Stock Publishers, 199 W. 8th Ave., Suite 3, Eugene, OR 97401.

Wipf & Stock
An Imprint of Wipf and Stock Publishers
199 W. 8th Ave., Suite 3
Eugene, OR 97401

www.wipfandstock.com

PAPERBACK ISBN: 978-1-4982-8235-2
HARDCOVER ISBN: 978-1-4982-8237-6
EBOOK ISBN: 978-1-4982-8236-9

Manufactured in the U.S.A.   JULY 31, 2017

Contents

Preface | vii
Introduction | ix

1. IPV in the Black Experience: The Problem | 1
2. The History of the Black Church in America | 22
3. The Theological Foundations that Support IPV in the Black Church | 42
4. Focus Group Interviews | 70
5. IPV Prevention in the Black Church | 95

Conclusion | 114
Bibliography | 119
Index | 127

Preface

THE PERENNIAL PROBLEM OF intimate partner violence (IPV) has gained national attention, which is indicative of the increased awareness efforts of advocates, law enforcement, government, education, and social service agencies. This awareness serves as the catalyst for the upsurge in legislation, law enforcement involvement, and incarceration of abusers. The issue of domestic violence has a significant impact on women who suffer intolerable mistreatment at the hands of their abusers. The motives for domestic abuse against women are grounded in power, control, and fear. Although the secular community has strategically increased awareness and implemented policies to combat abuse, the Black church continues to experience challenges implementing effective stratagems to address the issue and protect women. Therefore, it is imperative for the church to examine its current policies and practices utilized to address IPV against women. The Black church must continue to investigate why women are hesitant to report abuse and remain in abusive relationships.

The church must develop and incorporate a training protocol for pastors and church leaders to recognize the signs and symptoms of IPV and empower women to report abuse. The training will also deliver a component on the development of policies and the creation of a human resource department to embed domestic violence awareness and prevention within the church by-laws. Further, the training will serve to equip congregants to assist in the awareness campaign and prevention efforts to increase reporting of abuse. The church must also build a pragmatic, holistic, and collaborative partnership between the faith-based and advocate communities in order to address IPV, and to build a fence around victims and survivors to provide them with resources, provide services to assist victims who desire to flee abusive situations, and provide safe spaces for women not ready to report.

Introduction

First Lady Bonita James, affectionately known to her congregation as First Lady B., is an intelligent and compassionate woman who brings a sense of joy to any room with her contagious smile. She is a proud fourth-generation Church of God in Christ (hereafter referred to as COGIC) member who lived in the red hills of Georgia prior to her family relocating to New York City in 1986. She became a Christian at the age of fifteen. First Lady B. has two brothers and one sister, who served in their father's church, St. Matthew COGIC. Her younger brother, Thomas, served as the assistant pastor while her sister Mary served as the minister of music. The older brother, Michael, pastored his own congregation with his wife and family.

    First Lady B. met a handsome and debonair preacher named Delbert James, an ordained elder at a local COGIC, and soon married in a storybook wedding ceremony. Their family quickly grew in size with the birth of four children in an eight-year span, the purchase of a five-bedroom home in an upper-middle-class neighborhood, and an additional vehicle to support the new additions to the family. After Delbert entered into pastoral ministry, church membership grew rapidly in the first year—it was hailed as one of the fastest growing churches in the city. However, what began as the dream of a lifetime quickly turned into a nightmare. First Lady B. had strong reservations concerning meetings her husband conducted alone with women in the church, but would usually remain silent. The issue never subsided and grew more intense.

    First Lady B.'s concerns escalated after a heated confrontation in which she stood her ground, and after one such fight Pastor Delbert slapped her and left an imprint of his hand on her face. First Lady B. withdrew to her

Introduction

room and drenched her pillow with tears of shock and pain. In the past, he had only raised his voice; however, this was the first of many times that he engaged in physical violence. The experience grew worse as Pastor Delbert became more physically abusive as the encounters escalated through increasing verbal arguments, threats, and psychological and emotional abuse. However, the abuse was kept veiled from the presence of their children, family, and the congregation.

The James family was perceived as the perfect family, always smiling and interacting with congregants, dressed impeccably, and very well behaved when attending church and family events. Pastor Delbert continued to preach every Sunday and remained faithful to the sacerdotal duties of the church. Although he promised on many occasions to never hit First Lady B. again, the abuse continued for the next twenty-five years and only ended when Pastor Delbert breathed his last breath.

§

The notion of Intimate Partner Violence (hereafter referred to as IPV) has garnered a tremendous amount of national attention within the National Football League through the video of former Baltimore Ravens running back Ray Rice hitting his fiancée, now wife, Janay, in an Atlanta elevator. Further, other NFL stars have had charges of domestic violence filed against them, namely Ray McDonald of the San Francisco 49ers, Greg Hardy of the Carolina Panthers (now with the Dallas Cowboys), A. J. Jefferson of the Minnesota Vikings, Robert Reynolds of the Tennessee Titans, Dez Bryant of the Dallas Cowboys, and Rod Smith of the Denver Broncos. The theme among all the men listed above is their ethnicity—African American. The issues related to the NFL and the collective reaction to the video of Ray and Janay Rice has reignited a national conversation about IPV. Further, the video of Rice knocking Janay unconscious has generated discourse on the issues of abuse, power, and help for victims of IPV.

The notion of abuse of women in the faith-based community is immensely similar to that of the wives of NFL players listed above, as well as other women who suffer domestic abuse at the hands of abusers in general. IPV remains prevalent throughout the religious spectrum and affects women from diverse backgrounds, ages, and socioeconomic status. Although the true identity of First Lady B. and Delbert James have been kept confidential, the story of First Lady B. and thousands of women in the Black church is more common than most congregants, community members,

Introduction

and clergy are willing to admit. The issue of domestic abuse, in most cases, is hidden deep within the hearts of women, tucked away from the pastor and leadership of the church as women silently suffer.

The role of religion, spirituality, and community is immensely sacrosanct to the Black church, from the dark era of slavery through today in the twenty-first century. The Black community in the United States has always been grounded in the notions of religion, spirituality, and the church as the foundation for communal living and social justice. However, it is these same spiritual communities where change and reform must take place to significantly reduce domestic violence and assist women in reporting abuse. Although the focus of the book emphasizes the Black church, the intent is to acknowledge that the issue of domestic abuse has a wider application to nearly all Christian communities impacted by domestic violence.

Chapter 1 will be a discussion of the metrics, signs, symptoms, and risk factors for IPV. This chapter will also discuss the application for the Black community, especially the faith community, and the impact on children, families, and congregants. The chapter will also discuss the impact of abuse on Black women, including the intersection of stalking and domestic violence, the cycle of abuse phases, and the Power and Control Wheel. Understanding the impact of domestic violence in the Black church and community is imperative to comprehend the widespread problem in both sectors, but most importantly in the church, with the goal of exposing the problem and helping victims report abuse in lieu of masking the pain. Since historically the church has been the strongest and most autonomous institution in the Black community and family life, it is best suited for addressing the problem of IPV among its members.

Chapter 2 will discuss a brief history of the Black church in America from a Pentecostal perspective, and examine the roots of the Black church in America during the Jim Crow Era and Civil Rights Movement, and also examine the culture of the church in America. The chapter will discuss the role of Black males in the family and church, the role of the pastor, and the role of women in the family, church, and marriage. The chapter will also assist us in understanding how the history of the Black church and the historical roles of individuals in the church support abuse in the church, specifically male dominance as a vital construct.

Chapter 3 will help us understand the theological underpinnings and foundations that support IPV in the church, coupled with the lack of education among pastors particularly during slavery and the Jim Crow Era.

INTRODUCTION

This is imperative in providing the biblical interpretations and exegesis that were utilized to sustain abuse in the church. The chapter will briefly examine texts from the Old and New Testaments utilized by clergy and the church to subjugate and oppress women and uphold male dominance.

Chapter 4 will engage us in a discussion concerning why women remain apprehensive to report abuse and the impact of domestic violence on the family and congregation. The chapter will highlight conversations with women who have experienced abuse in the church by sharing their personal experiences with IPV and how they overcame trauma. The names and identities of the women will be kept strictly confidential, but their memories and stories are real. This chapter will provide insight into the mind of abuse victims and their courage to escape the abuse while continuing to work and care for their children.

Chapter 5 invites us to a discussion of IPV prevention and how pastors and church leaders can address the issue, including: addressing the hesitancy of women to report abuse; developing protocols for reporting abuse in the church as well as models of reporting, awareness, and education; creating a human resource department within the church utilizing the Temporary Assistance for Needy Families Domestic Violence Program (TA-DVS) as a model for the church to provide financial assistance to abuse victims; embedding IPV policy within church bylaws; developing a holistic methodology for combating family violence; and building a fence of safety and protection for abuse victims.

Chapter 6 will provide a summary of the work with recommendations for the Black church to consider in addressing abuse, helping women to report, and developing internal church and ministry policies to protect victims who disclose. The goal of the chapter is to inspire the church to take the pole position against domestic violence and become one of the leaders in providing assistance for victims. The chapter will also make a clarion call for prophetic voices within the church to step forward and collectively cry out against violence and build a coalition of advocates that remain relentless in their effort to significantly reduce occurrences of violence while encouraging women and victims to report abuse.

Chapter 1

IPV in the Black Experience: The Problem

Intimate Partner Violence is not confined to a specific culture, ethnicity, race, religion, age, or socioeconomic context; IPV does not discriminate and is clearly perceived in nearly every facet of life.[1] The notion of abuse is depicted as the continuation of unwanted behaviors ranging from verbal abuse, physical abuse, financial abuse, oppression, subjugation, sexual assault, rape, and homicide. Further, domestic violence often combines verbal, physical, emotional, psychological, financial, and sexual abuse with the goal to control, inflict fear, subjugate, and dominate individuals, particularly women.[2] Domestic abuse is certainly not a new issue, however, the time has come for a coalition of private and public entities to join forces to revise and develop new solutions to address the increasing problem and encourage victims to report early and often.

The methodology of abusers is to devalue victims by utilizing derogatory statements that conjure feelings of negativity, implementing bullying tactics to imply that victims are insane, engaging in mind-game strategies, utilizing guilt and humiliation as weapons of control, and treating victims as slaves while functioning as owner or master. Further, IPV victims are often perceived as sex objects and purchased property subject to abusive and controlling tactics of abusers who control all aspects of the relationship, define and enforce rules, and make or carry out threats.

Abusers threaten to harm themselves if victims leave, threaten to harm the victim's family and/or pets, and threaten to report victims to police or

1. Garcia and Patrick, *Gendered Justice*, 45–64.
2. Shipway, *Domestic Violence*, 1.

child services.[3] Further, the underfunctioning personality of abusers is manifested in their unwillingness to contribute physically or emotionally to the relationship or system, requiring others to regularly act on their behalf. Interpersonal violence is prevalent in all racial and ethnic backgrounds, socioeconomic statuses, religions, faiths, and church sizes; there is virtually no one on earth that is exempt from experiencing domestic abuse either directly or indirectly. Although the issue permeates through the vicissitudes of life, the emphasis of this book will focus on domestic violence in the Black church and community and discuss why victims in this demographic are apprehensive to report. The notion of abuse remains a grave issue and the time has arrived to provide victims with the necessary tools to increase reporting.

The book will also examine the history and methodology of the Black church and its handling of abuse issues that encouraged women to remain in abusive marriages and relationships. This is an important aspect to examine as many women, including First Lady B., have been encouraged to stand by their man due to his position and role in the church. Women in the Black church have been encouraged to pray, fast, read Scripture, and trust in the Lord while suffering abuse in the name of Jesus, holding the church together (by not reporting), and protecting the husbands who have abused them. The time has come for the church to emerge as a leading faith-based institution to combat domestic abuse at a higher level by developing internal policies and external relationships that will assist in increasing reports of abuse, provide women with more options, and significantly reduce the occurrences of domestic violence. Although the Black church is generally concerned about abuse, it can no longer perceive IPV as a spiritual issue with physical manifestations, but must see it as an issue that impacts women who need assistance from the church.

The Religion and Violence e-Learning Project (RAVE) provides compelling data regarding IPV and women in the church:

- 95 percent of women in the church report that they have never heard a specific message on abuse preached from the pulpit in their church.
- 58 percent have helped an abused woman while one in four have offered a victim a bed for a night.
- 69.8 percent of women have sought the help of someone in their church regarding a family or related issue, and many women who

---

3. Haley and Braun-Haley, *War on the Home Front*, 103–5.

have experienced IPV, do not feel that the term "abused" is applicable to them.

- 9.3 percent of pastors have counseled five or more abused women within the last year.
- 83.2 percent of pastors state they have counseled at least one abused woman.
- 8 percent feel equipped to respond to domestic violence while 31 percent state that they have preached a message on abuse.
- 40 percent state that they discuss IPV in premarital counseling.
- 74 percent of pastors underestimate the level of domestic abuse in their congregations, and when they attempt to address the issue they often do more harm than good.
- 65 percent of pastors have only spoken once about IPV within the past year.[4]

The majority of pastors do not consider sexual abuse or domestic violence central to larger religious themes. For the pastors who said they have spoken about the topic, 72 percent said they did so because they believed it was a problem in their local communities, compared to the 25 percent who said they spoke out because they felt it was a problem in their congregations.[5] Al Miles stated that after conducting 158 interviews with pastors, most were in denial about abuse in their congregations and the fact that victims and abusers attend their services each week.[6] Although some pastors were not aware of the severity of abuse in the congregation, most stated that they would not hesitate to address the issue if they had the proper training and resources.[7]

According to the U.S. Religious Landscape Survey conducted in 2007 by the Pew Research Center's Forum on Religion and Public Life, Black Americans remain markedly more religious than the U.S. population as a whole.[8] Further, according to the Pew Research for Religion and Public Life Project, 87 percent of Black Americans describe themselves as belonging to one religious group or another and maintain a high level of affiliation with

4. Rave Project, "Looking at the Data . . . from Church Women."
5. Verdal, "Broken Silence."
6. Miles, *Domestic Violence*, 19–20.
7. Ibid.
8. BlackDemographics.com, "Black Church."

religion by attending prayer and religious services.[9] Additionally, nearly 80 percent of Blacks state that religion plays a very important role in their daily lives, as compared to 56 percent of all U.S. adults.

Further, 53 percent of Black Americans attend religious services once per week, with more than 76 percent reporting that they pray on a daily basis and 88 percent stating that they are absolutely certain that God exists. Although 72 percent of Blacks state that they are unaffiliated with a particular faith, most say that religion plays at least a minor role in their lives.[10] The metrics noted here are consequential for our study as they illustrate the direct link between African Americans and religious faith.

The Black church remains an integral part of the community, from the early years of slavery through the formation of the first Black churches in America, the Azusa Street Revival, the Civil Rights Movement, the post-Civil Rights era, and into the twenty-first century. The notions of faith and religion play an important role in the daily lives of Blacks; however, it must be noted that although specific IPV data fails to identify religious affiliation, there is evidence that abuse exists in the church because the membership of the church is comprised of community members who regularly participate in religious practice.

In today's society, domestic violence receives a plethora of media attention when professional athletes, celebrities, entertainers, politicians, and millionaire moguls are involved or charged with assault and abuse. The widely covered domestic violence case involving Ray Rice has sparked fury and perhaps rage from media journalists, sports analysts, and politicians; even President Barack Obama made remarks on the issue and criticized the NFL's handling of the incident. The president commented that stopping domestic violence is bigger than football and everyone has a responsibility to put a stop to it. Although the president displayed disdain for abuse, his comments were just one among many that more than likely failed to have a major impact on ending abuse.

The metrics in this section will capture the perennial and vast issue of abuse as a problem much larger than the Ray and Janay Rice incident and many other widely publicized occurrences of abuse, whether it involves a professional athlete, entertainer, politician, mogul, clergyman, or community leader.

---

9. Pew Research Center, "Religious Portrait of African Americans."
10. Ibid.

IPV in the Black Experience: The Problem
Metrics for Domestic Violence

In a 1995–1996 study conducted in all U.S. states and the District of Columbia, a survey of sixteen thousand men and women regarding IPV concluded that:

- Nearly 76 percent of women, compared to 25 percent of men, have been raped or physically assaulted by a current or former spouse, cohabiting partner, date partner, or acquaintance at some point during their life.[11]
- In the United States, approximately 1.3 million women as compared to 835,000 men are physically assaulted by a partner each year.[12]
- IPV accounted for 20 percent of all non-fatal violent crime in 2001.[13]
- In 2002, of females who were murdered with a firearm, two thirds were murdered by an intimate partner.
- The number of females shot and killed by their husbands and intimate partners was three times higher than the total number murdered by male strangers using all weapons combined as compared to single victim/single offender incidents in 2002.[14]
- Males comprised 83 percent of spouse murderers and 75 percent of date murderers.
- 50 percent of offenders in state prison for spousal abuse killed their victims; wives were more likely than husbands to be killed by their spouses; and wives were about half of all spouses in the population in 2002 but were 81 percent of all persons killed by their spouse.[15]
- Based upon a report from ten countries, between 55 percent and 95 percent of women who have been physically abused by their partners have never contacted a non-governmental agency.
- More than 1,500 women are killed per year in the United States.[16]

---

11. Tjaden and Thoennes, "Extent, Nature, and Consequences."
12. Ibid.
13. Rennison, "Intimate Partner Violence," 1.
14. Violence Policy Center, "When Men Murder Women."
15. Durose et al., "Family Violence Statistics," 31–32.
16. Gelles, *Intimate Violence in Families*, 70–78.

- Approximately every nine seconds a woman is assaulted or beaten. Domestic violence is the leading cause of injury for women, above car accidents, muggings, and rape combined.[17]
- One in every four women is at risk of experiencing domestic violence.[18]
- 75 percent of domestic violence victims are women.[19]

Although the data clearly confirms that women experience abuse, assault, harm, and injury at a much higher rate than men, it is important to note that men experience IPV at the hands of women. The Centers for Disease Control (CDC) concluded that, based upon a 2010 national survey, more men were victims of IPV and over 40 percent of severe physical violence is directed towards men. Further, the 2010 survey concluded that men were more likely to experience abuse in the form of psychological aggression and control over sexual or reproductive health.[20]

The CDC study conducted by the National Intimate Partner and Sexual Violence Survey (NISVS) is strikingly different from the National Violence Against Women Survey (NVAWS). The NISVS concedes that it failed to measure the ratio of male to female victims of IPV, while the NVAWS survey measured severe physical violence against men.[21]

Although there is evidence that males experience IPV by women, the data overwhelmingly confirms that women experience domestic violence by men at a much higher rate.

Metrics for Black Women and IPV

Black Americans, specifically, Black women, suffer deadly violence from family members at a rate decidedly higher than any other social group in America. Blacks experience victimization by intimate partners and IPV at a rate 35 percent higher than that of their White female counterparts and twenty-two times higher than other ethnicities.[22] Black women experience domestic violence at the highest rate between the ages of twenty to twenty-four. While Black women experience similar levels of victimization in all

17. CDC, "Costs of Intimate Partner Violence against Women."
18. Ibid.
19. Tjaden and Thoennes, "Extent, Nature, and Consequences."
20. Hoff, "CDC Study."
21. Ibid.
22. Rennison and Welchans, "Intimate Partner Violence."

other categories compared to White women, they experience abuse at a slightly higher rate.[23] Further, 40 percent of Black women report some type of coercive contact of a sexual nature by age eighteen, and the number one killer between the ages of fifteen and thirty-four is homicide at the hands of a current or former intimate partner.[24]

The Intersection of Stalking and IPV

The notion of stalking is intertwined with abuse as most women are stalked by abusers, especially on college campuses. Stalking is depicted as a course of behavior conducted directly or indirectly toward an individual with the intent to cause fear and harm. Stalking can be immensely serious, escalate over time, and end in violence.[25]

Stalking involves, directly or indirectly, repeated, unwanted, intrusive, and frightening communications from the perpetrator by phone, mail, or email.[26] The profiles of stalkers and abusers are strikingly similar and involve use of the same fear tactics against their victims. The intersection of stalking and IPV is vital to this discussion, as most victims have some knowledge of their stalker or abuser.[27] Although not all stalking and abuse incidents occur in the same place, such as home, work, or school, the intersection must be noted as serious cases of domestic violence most often involve some form of stalking.[28]

The victims of IPV, in most cases, are also victims of stalking and most victims experience this at the hands of a current or former spouse, current or former cohabitating partner, or current or former dating partner.[29] Further, 81 percent of women that have been stalked by an intimate partner have also been physically assaulted by the same partner, and 31 percent of women stalked by an intimate partner have been sexually assaulted by the same partner.[30] Although men experience stalking at an almost equal rate to women in certain categories, the distinction of stalking between men

---

23. Ibid.
24. Harvard Black Law Students Association, "Domestic Violence—Sad Facts."
25. Stalking Resource Center, "Stalking."
26. Ibid.
27. Mullen, Pathé, and Purcell, *Stalkers and Their Victims*, 35–46.
28. Ibid.
29. http://www.fcasv.org.
30. Ibid.

and women centers on the issue of power and control, with men possessing more power and control over women in regards to stalking and violence.[31]

Signs and Symptoms of IPV

It is essential to understand the signs and symptoms of IPV in the fight to stop occurrences of abuse, power, control, and oppression of women. The signs and symptoms usually manifest after the honeymoon phase of the relationship, start small, and ultimately progress into abusive and controlling behavior, implanting a high level of fear in women so they remain in the abusive relationship rather than seek assistance.

Further, more and more research suggests that the signs and symptoms of IPV manifest during the dating period as well.[32] Due to the underfunctioning nature of abusers, most victims blame themselves for the abuse and develop tactics to avoid further incidents in lieu of reporting. There are many signs and symptoms of IPV, with fear and anxiety being the most telling behaviors abused women exhibit. The sign of an abusive relationship can be discovered in perhaps the most revealing behavior of victims: fear of their spouse or partner when in their presence or in anticipation of the interaction with their spouse or partner when they arrive home.

Another sign of IPV may be the avoidance of certain topics of discussion for fear of angering or upsetting the spouse or partner. Further, a victim may feel they are unable to correctly perform certain functions and tasks for their spouse or partner because they believe they deserve to be hurt or mistreated. Thus, victims continue to struggle psychologically with believing they are the problem in the relationship and blame themselves for all negative aspects of the relationship while assigning all positive actions to the abuser.[33]

In addition to this, abusers threaten and attempt to hurt the victim by injuring or killing them, threatening to take children away, or stating that victims will never see their children again. Abusers coerce or force victims to engage in copulation or perform non-consensual sexual acts and threaten to carry out the act of destroying property, utilizing manipulative and convincing behaviors and threats of suicide if the victim leaves the

---

31. Ibid.
32. Miles, *Ending Violence in Teen Dating Relationships*, 20–21.
33. Ibid.

marriage or relationship.[34] Further, abusers exhibit degrading, derogatory, and belittling behaviors, inclusive of constant humiliation.

This is coupled with unnecessary and excessive criticism, treating the victim so badly that they are embarrassed to be in the presence of family and friends, and ignoring the accomplishments and devaluing the opinions of victims, perceiving them as an object and property rather than a person.[35] The controlling behavior of abusers is a key factor in instilling fear and anxiety into the minds of victims. In the perception of victims, controlling behaviors are the common tools of abusers and these behaviors become tactics to subjugate, oppress, and control women. The controlling behaviors of abusers include acting excessively jealous or possessive of victims, stalking victims by monitoring activities, preventing victims from seeing friends and family, and limiting victims' access to money, phone, or cars.[36]

Cycle of Abuse

At this juncture, it is important to discuss the cycle of abuse to further understand the mind of an abuser and the manipulative behavior utilized to dominate women and prevent them from reporting IPV.

---

34. Kennedy-Dugan and Hock, *It's My Life Now*, o.
35. Evans, *Verbally Abusive Relationship*, 8–11.
36. Ibid.

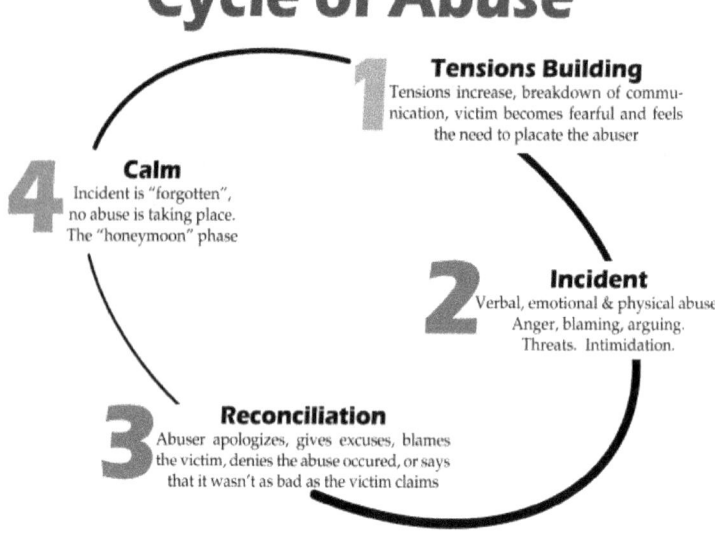

Image 1: Cycle of Abuse[37]

The cycle of abuse[38] was introduced by Lenore Walker in 1979 to explain the pattern of behaviors in abusive relationships based upon her interviews with 1,500 women who experienced abuse in relationships.[39] Some might state that the model is too simplistic, cannot be universally applied, and the data is primarily anecdotal. However, Walker's model was hailed as revolutionary and is still utilized by a myriad of national IPV organizations.[40]

The cycle of abuse is demarcated into four phases: *tension building, acting out, reconciliation*, and *calm*. These phases generally follow one another in order and are repeated until the IPV ends when the victim abandons the marriage or relationship, or by intervention. The cycle of abuse can occur numerous times in abusive relationships, with the total cycle lasting from a few hours to a few months.

The cycle typically happens no matter how hard victims attempt to prevent it. Further, as the length of the cycle of abuse diminishes over time, the reconciliation and calm phases are replaced by time, violence, control,

37. Bancroft, *Why Does He Do That?*, 8–11.
38. Walker, *Battered Woman Syndrome* (1984), 14–33.
39. McCue, *Domestic Violence* (1995), 62–63.
40. Dutton and Golant, *Batterer*, 39–58.

and abuse. The Jefferson College of Health Sciences (JCHS) provides detailed information regarding each phase of the cycle of abuse that will give further insight into the minds of abusers.

Tension-Building Phase

The tension-building phase of the cycle of abuse depicts the behavior of abusers who become extremely edgy, resulting in negative behaviors and frustrations. The tension continues to build and increase to the level in which abusers experience feelings of losing control over the behavior and actions of victims. The reactions of abusers to potentially negative circumstances include moodiness, withdrawal of love and affection, constant condemnation, devaluing the victim, threatening, and speaking to victims in an elevated and demeaning tone. The reactions of victims in the tension-building phase include attempts to calm the abuser and stop abuse, fulfill the role of nurturer, completely withdraw from activities, and feelings of daily apprehension, whether in or out of the presence of the abuser. This is described as the "walking on egg shells phase."[41]

Acting-Out/Acute Explosion Phase

The JCHS renames this phase "acute explosion" rather than "acting out," and it is often the most diminutive stage, as violence regularly occurs at this juncture with the outward expression of more anger.

At this phase, victims detach themselves from the abuser to prevent triggering more violence; the acute explosion phase generally ends after a violent eruption by the abuser. The abuser will likely populate this phase with physical abuse, rape, emotional violence, humiliation, demeaning language, and the potential use of weapons. The victim will generally react with self-protection; calling law enforcement, family, or friends; attempting to calm the abuser using reason and logic; fighting back; or withdrawing.[42]

---

41. Jefferson College of Health Sciences, "Cycle of Abuse in Relationships."
42. Ibid.

Reconciliation

The reconciliation phase is typically a more welcomed stage by both the abuser and the victim. The abuser usually expresses remorse for their actions and the victim starts to believe that the abuser can change. This stage often continues until the abuser begins to feel confident and gains the victim's trust, but then starts to feel a loss of control over the victim's behavior. This stage has been shown to decrease in length over time and in some cases it can disappear entirely. The behaviors and reactions of abusers in this stage include promising to get help, asking for forgiveness, buying gifts for victims, promising to love and cherish victims, and starting a new life free and clear of abuse. The reactions for victims include agreeing to stay, attending individual and family counseling, experiencing feelings of happiness, and exhibiting hopeful behavior that the issue has improved.[43]

The Calm Phase

The calm phase can be perceived as an extension of the reconciliation phase and evokes an atmosphere of peace. During this phase, the abuser may verbally commit to attend individual and marriage therapy, request forgiveness from the victim, and present a normal family atmosphere. The calm stage also includes the abuser purchasing gifts and presents, even engaging in loving copulation. However, due to the nature of abusive relationships, when the calm phase ends, the tension rebuilds, leading to acts of explosion by the abuser, then to reconciliation, and back to the calm phase.[44]

The cycle of abuse in relationships is the foundation for studying IPV and was groundbreaking for advocates to provide not only a framework, but a voice from the professional ranks to validate the issue from a medical and academic perspective. The cycle of abuse paved the trajectory for the Power and Control Wheel, which has become the most commonly used image in IPV trainings. The Power and Control Wheel outlines the various tactics utilized by abusers and the impact on victims. The information is extensive and insightful for advocates and should be placed in plain view in every church around the country. The Power and Control Wheel is an important tool that the faith-based community can utilize to encourage victims to report abuse. It demonstrates the cycle of abuse further and depicts the twin

---

43. Ibid.
44. Ibid.

IPV in the Black Experience: The Problem

notions of power and control that abusers utilize to oppress, abuse, and dominate women. The Power and Control Wheel, shown below, is a helpful apparatus for individuals to understand the overall pattern of abusive and violent behavior that abusers use to maintain control over women.

Image 2: Power and Control Wheel[45]

The wheel begins with behaviors of intimidation such as looks, actions, brandishing weapons, and gestures, followed by coercion and threats, such as threats to commit suicide, leaving the victim and family, or co-contacting Child Protective Services (CPS) if women fail to comply with demands. The wheel also presents the aspect of male privilege in which the abuser forces women into subjugation through defining the roles of men and women, making all major household decisions, committing economic

---

45. Domestic Abuse Intervention Programs, "Wheel Gallery."

abuse, and attempting to prevent women from working to limit their access to people who could possibly help them.

The Power and Control Wheel provides insight into the methodologies utilized by abusers to manipulate women into believing that the abuse is not as bad as it appears, thus minimizing the impact of abuse, potentially blaming women for IPV, and failing to take the woman's concerns seriously.[46] The wheel continues with emotional abuse and isolation as chief tactics to depress and discourage women by devaluing their image and persona while exercising ultimate control of all outside activity, inclusive of visiting family and friends, and certain publications the victim reads. The Power and Control Wheel is a resourceful tool to help comprehend the methodology and tactics that abusers employ to subjugate and abuse women, especially women in the church.[47] The church must understand the nature of these controlling behaviors and communicate this in trainings, seminars, and educational sessions to ensure that women recognize the schemes of abusive men.

Christians, in some cases, understand the spiritual impact of abuse but fail to understand the non-spiritual issues related to IPV. It is imperative to understand that abuse is mainly about control rather than about anger or physical violence. Therefore, disciples of the church must be cognizant and refrain from neglecting the non-spiritual issues in lieu of the spiritual aspect of domestic abuse.

Risk Factors for IPV

Understanding the risk factors associated with domestic violence will help pastors and leaders frame and analyze questions, determine effective measures, recognize key intervention points, and select appropriate responses.

Risk factors do not automatically indicate that a person will be controlled by an abuser; however, understanding risk factors can help pastors educate and equip women with resources when they are ready to escape IPV situations.

---

46. Ibid.
47. Ibid.

IPV in the Black Experience: The Problem

Socioeconomic Status

To understand the plight of domestic violence victims, we must recognize their economic position in American culture. Over half of homeless families nationally are Black even though they comprise 12 percent of the total population. Moreover, the U.S. Census Bureau found that while 28 percent of White female-headed households in 1998 were below the poverty line, 40 percent of female households headed by Black women were below the poverty line. To better clarify, the median annual income for a White woman in 1996 was $11,266 and the median income for Black women was $9,508; this has not changed in today's society. IPV victims of lower socioeconomic status have fewer resources compared to IPV victims who have more resources.[48]

Christopher Devery conducted a study that concluded that socioeconomic status is not an indicator of domestic violence for three reasons. The first reason is that the theoretical perspective that has informed much of the research and comments are inconclusive of the relationship between socioeconomic status and IPV. Secondly, the influence of public awareness campaigns has stressed that IPV impacts all women. Thirdly, there is a stark contrast and differing interpretations of the empirical research on abuse and socioeconomic status.[49]

Although Devery believes that the relationship between domestic violence and socioeconomic status is minimal, the metrics overwhelmingly support the link between socioeconomic status and domestic abuse.

Sarah Knapton stated in an article that highlighted a study by Heidi Fischer Bjelland, a PhD student at the Norwegian Police University College, that in some cases where women earned at least 67 percent of the total household income they were more likely to suffer or experience psychological and physical abuse. Bjelland argued that wherever power is unevenly allocated in a relationship, the likelihood of abuse increases significantly and violence and control is utilized to compensate for the weak position of the abuser. She further commented that her study indicates that high income and education can work as a protection against IPV as long as the income of the women does not exceed that of the male partner.[50] Flowers and Kauiken state that it would appear far-fetched that women with high incomes and societal status

---

48. Martinson, "Analysis of Racism and Resources," 260–70.
49. Bureau of Crime and Research Statistics, "Crime & Socioeconomic Status."
50. Knapton, "Educated and Well-Paid Women."

would be abused, but also agree with Bjelland that the higher the income for women, the more they are trapped by the same resource. They state that most women desire to continue their lives as normal as possible to prevent shame and negative reactions from the community. Although women of all socioeconomic backgrounds experience IPV, women of lower socioeconomic backgrounds are many more times at risk due to poverty and factors such as stress and resources for stress reduction, including leaving the situation.[51] White women tend to experience a different set of issues, as it is likely more arduous for them to flee domestic abuse because of socioeconomic status. However, Black women who fall into the lower socioeconomic brackets tend to be more likely victims of abuse as compared to White women, Hispanic women, and Asian women of the same socioeconomic level.

The National Poverty Center (NPC) concluded that:

- While approximately 15.1 percent of Americans experienced poverty, the poverty rate among Blacks was 27.4 percent as compared to 9.9 percent of Whites and 12.1 percent of Asians.
- Further, poverty rates were highest among Black and Hispanic women who were single heads of households.[52]

The National Center for Law and Economic Justice states that in 2012:

- There were more than 46.5 million people living in poverty, with an average yearly household income of less than $23,492.
- 27.2 percent of Blacks were living in poverty as compared to non-Hispanic Whites and were three times more likely to live in deep poverty.[53]

Further, the U.S. Census reported that between 2007 and 2011:

- 43 out of the 50 states had poverty rates above 20 percent for Blacks.
- Iowa, Maine, Mississippi, and Wisconsin had poverty rates above 35 percent for Blacks.
- Only six states (Alaska, Delaware, Hawaii, Maryland, New Jersey, and Virginia) had poverty rates of 20 percent or less for Blacks.[54]

---

51. Browne, "Violence in Marriage," 54–55.
52. National Poverty Center, "Poverty in the United States."
53. Ibid.
54. Macartney, Bishaw, and Fontenot, "American Community Survey Briefs."

Socioeconomic status is an important factor that confirms that Black women of lower socioeconomic status who are victims of IPV are more likely than middle- and upper-class White women who are victims of domestic violence to need "extensive services and support" in order to leave an abusive relationship.

Socioeconomic status is defined in terms of income, education, and occupation.[55] Although White women have difficulty leaving abusive relationships as well, Black women have limited access to financial resources, while White women stay because of community status. Socioeconomic status plays an important factor in the Black community and establishes a clear link between the two concepts. The church must understand this crucial link and how it relates to congregants who are more susceptible to occurrences of abuse as compared to other ethnic and non-ethnic groups based upon socioeconomic status. The victims of lower socioeconomic status have fewer resources in addressing IPV issues as compared to victims who have more resources.

Race/Ethnicity

Black women experience IPV at rates 35 percent higher than their White counterparts and two and half times the rate of women of other races and men.[56] Black Americans account for a disproportionate number of intimate partner homicides, and in 2005 Black Americans accounted for almost one third of the intimate partner homicides in this country.[57] This threat has disproportionately dire consequences for Black women, as the social construct of race/ethnicity plays a great role in domestic violence and abuse.[58]

There are other risk factors that contribute, such as neighborhood, pregnancy, education, and prior abuse; however, socioeconomic status and race/ethnicity are the most significant. The church must be cognizant of these risk factors in order to address the issue of domestic violence in a way that is supportive of victims and families.

---

55. Carlson, Harris, Holden, "Violence in the African American Family."
56. Hampton and Gelles, "Violence toward Black Women."
57. Thompson, "Partner Violence, Social Support."
58. Hampton, Oliver, and Magarian, "Domestic Violence in the African American Community."

Impact of IPV on Black Children

The impact of IPV on Black children grows worse with each incident of abuse, given that poverty and race are risk factors. Children experience a tremendous amount of anxiety and post-traumatic stress disorder (PTSD) as a result of observing and experiencing domestic violence. In the absence of intervention, children are at severe risk for delinquency, substance abuse, low educational achievement, and an inability to foster good relationships. Children who witness abuse in the home are nine times more likely to abuse or accept abuse, perpetuate the cycle, in addition to other personal and societal costs.[59] Further, Black male children who are exposed to domestic violence in the home at an early age are at greater risk of emulating abusive behaviors such as bullying relatives and non-relatives in their age category (whether male or female) and their intimate partners.[60] When children demonstrate behaviors of abuse in certain social settings, it is a clear manifestation of internal issues that children may not be able to articulate. Some of the symptoms include, but are not limited to: academic failure, sleep difficulties, avoidance of peer relationships, rebellious behavior, low self-esteem, threatening behavior, cruelty to pets and animals, and oppositional defiant behavior.[61]

IPV witnessed by teen girls in the home can serve as a catalyst for developing relationships with abusive men. This can have a grave impact on children and serious implications that perpetuate the cycle of abuse.[62]

IPV in the Black Church

The problem of IPV in the Black church has quietly elevated to one of the most important issues that the Black community must address and overcome. The issue of abuse in the church from the time period of 1930 to 2004 was mostly reticent and unreported; this led to a perennial cycle of abuse that dared victimized women to expose family violence. This perpetuation of domestic violence in the church is deeply embedded in the cultural and historical traditions of marriage and the ideology of the family

---

59. Buzawa, Buzawa, and Stark, *Responding to Domestic Violence*, 47–49.

60. Kaslow, Thorn, and Paranjpe, "Interventions for Abused African American Women," 47–58.

61. Walker, *Battered Woman Syndrome* (2000), 77–88.

62. Sanders, *Teen Dating Violence*, 27–37.

structure.[63] Although this book emphasizes IPV in the Black church, the intent is to acknowledge that the issue has a wider application to nearly all Christian communities. Although little is known about the correlation between IPV experiences and Black church folk,[64] a recent study has shown that the connection between domestic violence and spirituality is receiving more attention as Black women turn to the church to address domestic abuse in lieu of social service agencies, non-profit organizations, and mental health providers.[65]

There are four factors that lead to the enablement of violence in the Black church that have left many women paralyzed, helpless, petrified of their husbands, and hesitant to report.

The first factor that leads to the continuation of IPV in the Black church is the expectation of wives to honor and uphold their cultural and historical traditions, even at the costly expense of suffering perennial abuse. Women have committed themselves to the cultural tradition of soundless suffering, confiding only in God when the abuse is overwhelming.

The second factor that leads to the enablement of IPV in the Black church is the cultural and historical tradition of wives protecting their husbands to prevent the church from splitting and to keep their families together. The women have been encouraged to pray while being abused in hopes that God would work a miracle and transform the behavior of their abusive husbands, many of whom have served in church positions, including senior pastor, associate minister, or head deacon. Further, wives have been strongly encouraged to refrain from the deviation of this long-standing tradition, hearing stories from other pastors' wives who have "stayed there" and accepted the abuse in lieu of escaping the pain and suffering.

The third factor points to the nature and structure of the family. This structure is based upon a hierarchy in which the husband is the head of the household and the position of the wife is subordinate to the husband. In my interview with Pastor Michael Williams, he stated that a wife is expected to obey her husband in all things and rarely question his authority.[66] In the early twentieth century, Black women were encouraged to keep silent in the church, keep their homes well, take good care of the children, and

---

63. Johnson, *African American Christianity*, 57.
64. Martin and Martin, *Spirituality and the Black Helping Tradition*, 45.
65. Hassouneh-Phillips, "Strength and Vulnerability."
66. Interview with Pastor Michael Williams, House of Prayer for All Nations, May 29, 2014.

please their husbands at any cost. Thus, the value of women was minute and their roles in the community were parochial, as compared to men, who were perceived to be on the same level with God. They were never to be questioned, just obeyed.[67]

The last factor leading to the continuation of IPV emphasizes the concepts of community, belonging, and kinship, which are imperative and vital to the Black church. Humanity is defined as one belonging to a community, and religion is not an isolated aspect of humanity: it is woven into the fabric of every aspect of life. The role of religion and community is incredibly sacred to the Black church. There is virtually no such idea of individualism; religion, church, and community are intertwined and to think of oneself in isolation to the church community is, in some cases, equivalent to sin.[68] Further, this ideology of church and community is deeply embedded and has its roots in the dark era of slavery. During this bleak time in American history, Blacks were intentionally separated from their families; mothers painfully watched their sons be sold to slave owners across state lines, their daughters became housemaids and caregivers to slave owners' families, and their husbands were lynched and made examples to others who resisted enslavement. The increased cognizance of domestic violence has a plethora of champions in faith-based, governmental, non-profit, judicial, and law enforcement organizations, which continue to provide assistance to women, children, and abusers who embrace transformation and to prosecute abusers who fail to discontinue abusing.[69]

IPV has become one of the most prevailing social issues in American society today. Although many individuals have drawn the line in the sand against abuse, the question still looms with regard to the Black church and its ability to partner with the broader community to aggressively address the issue among their congregants.

Historically, the Black church has not been on the vanguard of the issue of IPV, and in most cases continues to struggle addressing the problem in the twenty-first century. Although there is recognition that Black church leaders have made some progress, much work is still needed to end family violence. The church must position itself to address domestic abuse and embark on the journey of awareness to policy development. The cavity between awareness and policy development must be closed by inculcating

67. Wallace, *Womanist Legacy of Trauma, Grief, and Loss*, 21.
68. Costen, *African American Worship*, 35.
69. Schewe, *Preventing Violence in Relationships*, 263–66.

leaders and congregants via training regarding the signs and symptoms of abuse, constructing healthy models that encourage parishioners and especially pastors' wives to report, embedding policy within church bylaws and human resource handbooks, and educating future generations on healthy marriage principles to help reduce domestic violence in the Black church.

Conclusion

Although there is need for additional study, the metrics and data for IPV are numerous and depict the severity of the problem, which continues to increase and multiply in society and the Black church. The faith-based community must be cognizant of the depth of the issue and the impact to female congregants, children, and families. The notion of abuse must also be inclusive of addressing the issues of the power struggle between victims and abusers, as well as providing help for the marginalized and powerless.

The church, specifically males who abuse, have in some cases lost the fervor to love their neighbor as themselves. The next chapter will help us identify how the passion to love our neighbor as we love ourselves was lost from a historical perspective as we discuss the roots of the Black church.

Chapter 2

The History of the Black Church in America

THE BLACK CHURCH IN America has a profound history. The Black church has significantly advanced in the spheres of economics, social justice, prominence, leadership, and membership as compared to the days of slavery, racism, and oppression. The church continues to grow exponentially, producing megachurches, multimillion-dollar ministries, first-class accommodations, and luxurious palates. The Oxygen Network airs the new reality show *Preachers of L.A.*, which captures the personal lives of famous Black preachers such as Pastor Wayne Chaney, Bishop Ron Gibson, Pastor Dietrich Haddon, Bishop Noel Jones, and Bishop Clarence E. McClendon.

The Pentecostal faith-based community gained international attention during the Azusa Street Revival and Civil Rights Movement, but remained subordinate to the White church. Black congregations have grown into vast corporate organizations and have catapulted to astronomical heights, with church leaders such as Pastor Creflo Dollar, Bishop I. V. Hilliard, Bishop T. D. Jakes, Bishop Eddie Long, and Pastor Fredrick K. C. Price reporting memberships of twenty to thirty thousand parishioners. Further, the Black church is represented in all aspects of secular society and culture, and has a permanent seat at important tables in national politics. This is a far cry from the days of slavery and being considered three fifths of a person,[1] and separate but equal—during the days when we were unworthy to ride in the front of the bus. The Black church no longer rides in the back of the bus; they ride in Bentleys, Phantom Rolls Royces, Mercedes, and BMWs.

---

1. Three fifths of a person was a compromise between Northern and Southern states during the Constitutional Convention of 1787 regarding how slaves would be counted when determining a state's total population for legislation and taxation purposes.

The History of the Black Church in America

Although most of the pastors listed on the previous page enjoy successful lives, it is fair to say that a portion of their income is earned from consultation services, speaking engagements and other economic ventures separate from the church. Megachurch pastors constantly endure the biased opinions of individuals with a parochial view into their lives and ministries. Further, most megachurches have established and developed effective ministries within the church to serve the needs of congregants; however, more work must be done to address the issue of domestic violence within Black congregations.

Understanding the history of the Black church is essential to understand the philosophy and methodology utilized to support a perennial hierarchical structure of power and control that subdues women, precludes IPV from being addressed, and leads to underreporting of abuse. Although the historical development of the Black church encompasses the African continent and nearly all Black denominations in America from the 1700s until today, our focus in this section will be on the historical aspect of the Black Pentecostal church in America as it specifically relates to the development, progression, and concentration of power, abuse, and control against women. This will help us understand the origin and paradigm of abuse and control, beginning with the roots of the Black church in America, as well as abuse, control, and power issues of European immigrants in Britain, the era of slavery, the Jim Crow era, and Civil Rights Movement. The discussion will demonstrate the overall mindset of Black men and the subjugation of women in the periods above.

Although we will discuss the historical aspect of the Black church and White male dominance in America beginning with slavery, the goal is not to drown our discussion with issues of race, but to help us recognize the patterns involved in the oppression of women that set the stage for IPV to develop and continue in the Black church.

Although Black congregants are members of Roman Catholic, Lutheran, Episcopal, Assembly of God, United Church of Christ, Church of Christ, Southern Baptist Convention, Conservative Baptist, and Church of God denominations, the highest concentrations of Black church membership are found primarily in the National Baptist Convention, African Methodist Episcopal (AME), African Methodist Zion Episcopal (AMEZ), Christian Methodist Episcopal (CME), Church of God in Christ (COGIC), and Apostolic Faith denominations. However, our focus will be on the Black Pentecostal aspect of the church.

Further, throughout the course of the book, when we use terms such as Black church, church, faith-based community, we, us, parishioners, God's people, congregants, Christians, Jesus followers, and disciples, it references the Black church in America. The formation and establishment of the Black church created a power block for pastors who held the authority to address abuse from the most powerful position in the church, the pulpit. This position of power has the ability to make an influential impact on how Christians perceive healthy marriages and relationships, domestic abuse, and men's attitudes toward females and femininity.

The roles of men, women, family, marriage, and pastors in the Black church are imperative in understanding the progression of abuse, power, and control as well as the unwritten rules within the congregation that support abuse and prevent victims from reporting. The church endured its own set of challenges with abuse and power during slavery, Jim Crow, the Civil Rights Movement, and the post-Civil Rights era; the church continues to fight racism, prejudice, and bigotry against the dominant culture. IPV in the Black church did not begin with issues of poverty, single-parent homes, or abusive homes. Although these are important indicators of the roots of abuse from a community perspective (and have been addressed in the previous chapter), the issue of domestic violence in the Black church centers on the placement of ultimate power in the hands of the pastor and chosen male leadership.

The concentration of power had its genesis in the standing tradition of male leadership to enforce silence and it prohibits victims and congregants from reporting domestic violence to church officials or law enforcement. The goal is to explore a brief historical depiction of the roots of the Black church in America without detracting from the core thought of the section. This historical piece is critical to trace the early development of the Black church and demonstrate the culture of male privilege and methods for holding women in submission that, in many cases, have led to abuse. Further, our goal will also demonstrate how males fail to view women as their neighbors, as needing help, nor do they view the issue of IPV from the lens of the marginalized.

Roots of the Black Church in America

The Black church developed rapidly in America out of the need to combat oppression, social injustice, and slavery, all of which promoted the White power structure and subjugated women, Blacks, Native American Indians, Mexicans, and other persons of color.[2] Although Blacks attend churches that were predominantly African American, Blacks were also members of churches in denominations such as the AME, AMEZ, Apostolic Faith, Pentecostal Assemblies of the World, Church of God in Christ, and the National Baptist Convention.[3]

The Black church in America has roots in the Roman Catholic Church. The Protestant Reformation movement that birthed the Black Pentecostal church in America has deep roots in the Pietistic movement that set the trajectory for the Methodist movement, a group of historically related denominations of Protestant Christianity founded by two brothers, John Wesley and Charles Wesley, and their friend George Whitefield.[4] Beginning with the early Methodist movement in America, Blacks were introduced to Christianity and the Methodist church eventually became the "religion" of many Black slaves. The AME church was founded by a Black preacher named Bishop Richard Allen, in Philadelphia in 1794. The AME church held its first convention in September 1830 in Philadelphia, shortly after the Cincinnati riots, when Whites attacked Blacks and destroyed their businesses. The AME convention was the first of its kind organized solely by Black church and community leaders.[5]

In 1870, the Colored Methodist Episcopal Church (now known as the Christian Methodist Episcopal Church, CME) was established in Jackson, Tennessee, by William Miles and Richard H. Vanderhost and grew from 40,000 to 67,000 members in three years.[6] In 1895, Black church officials established a new Baptist organization, the National Baptist Association, which was born out of a unification of three separate national conventions organized between 1880 and 1890.[7] In 1906, the Azusa Street Revival meeting held in Los Angeles and organized by William Seymour served as the launching pad for the Black Pentecostal church in America. Nearly all Black Pentecostal denominations in America can trace their foundation to the Azusa Street Revival and the spread of their organizations.[8] Although the

2. Harvey, "'That Was about Equalization after Freedom,'" 77–90.
3. Hill, *One Name but Several Faces*, 77.
4. Hammond, "John Wesley's Relations."
5. Strong, *American Methodism in the Nineteenth Century*, 63–72.
6. Dvorak, *African American Exodus*, 60–168.
7. Leonard, *Baptists in America*, 120–23.
8. Harvey, "Price of Discipleship," 30–32.

Black church experienced some limited freedom, Jim Crow laws continued to make circumstances immensely arduous for the Black parishioners in America.

The Jim Crow Era and the Black Church

Jim Crow laws were enacted during the years of 1876 through 1965 in America and enforced racial segregation in nearly all aspects of public life. Blacks held a separate but equal status in society and a position of inferiority to Whites. Jim Crow laws prohibited Blacks and Whites from occupying the same space in public, which extended to worshipping together in church services. However, Blacks were allowed to form separate congregations and worship together in peace without interruption from law enforcement.[9]

The first African American congregations in America were established by slaves and free Blacks in the 1800s in states such as Georgia, Kentucky, Pennsylvania, and Virginia. The oldest known Black church was founded by a slave named Peter Durret and his wife, who established the First African Church in Lexington, Kentucky, in 1790.[10] During the Great Awakening of the eighteenth century, Baptist and Methodist preachers travelled extensively throughout the South, conducting revival meetings and appealing to slaves, with many converting to Christianity and experiencing new freedom as a result of finding religion.[11] The churches that were established by slaves during the Great Awakening afforded Blacks the opportunity to experience a new level of respect as they served in very important positions such as preacher, pastor, and church leader.

Blacks were prohibited from serving in such positions in the Episcopalian and Anglican churches.[12] Prior to establishing their own congregations, Blacks were subjected to the worship styles and oversight of White slave masters as they continued to learn the foundations of the Christian faith. White slave masters held prayer services, Bible studies, and worship services on their plantations supervised by White representatives utilizing only specific Bible stories, specifically the curse of Ham and the Epistle of Philemon, to justify the ownership of slaves and reinforce obedience to slave

---

9. Berlin, *Making of African America*, 164–67.
10. National Park Service, "First African Baptist Church."
11. Melton, *Will to Choose*, 35–56.
12. Ibid.

masters.[13] However, the issues of racism, oppression, bigotry, and prejudice continued for the next eighty years, well into the Civil Rights Movement.

The power structure that was utilized to enslave Blacks combined politics, government at both the state and federal levels, and law enforcement to enforced laws of separate but equal and discrimination. Blacks, women, and all people of color had no access to this power structure dominated solely by White males. Although very minimal progress was made in America regarding civil rights, society still controlled the power structure and forced Blacks into oppression, subjugation, and denial of those rights. In addition to this, free White women were also victims of the dominance, abuse, power, and control of the White male power structure as they were not permitted to vote or hold positions of power in politics, church, or government.

The Women's Suffrage Movement of the 1920s galvanized many White women to form social groups to address the oppression and subjugation of women.[14] Further, they continued to experience great victories and progress in the Suffrage Movement, with some women being elected to the United States Congress, which led to the passing of the 19th Amendment, guaranteeing the right for women to vote. Although they were free due to the color of their skin, White women were still bound by the cultural traditions of the times, which extended into the Civil Rights Era.[15]

The Civil Rights Era and the Black Church

During the Civil Rights era, the Black church experienced significant growth and development and many well-known denominations were formed as a result of the outgrowth of the Azusa Street Revival.[16]

Black organizations such as the National Association for the Advancement of Colored People (NAACP), the Southern Christian Leadership Conference (SCLC), and the Urban League paved the way for the rise of the Black church through demonstrations, sit-ins, protests, and marches led by preachers and civic leaders. These actions were critical to growth; people rallied around the church and membership increased significantly.

---

13. Hopkins, *Down, Up, and Over*, 83–93.
14. Shouse, *Women's Rights*, 55–64.
15. Keyssar, *Right to Vote*, 139–75.
16. Ahlstrom, *Religious History of the American People*, 1059–60.

The churches in America served as major hubs to assemble in the fight against oppression. Leaders utilized their power and influence to gather thousands of parishioners together to fight the power structure of oppression. Reverend Dr. Martin Luther King Jr. and members of the SCLC played a key role in the struggle for civil rights.[17] In addition to this, the Civil Rights Movement featured leaders who were not clergyman such as James Meredith, Medgar Evers, Asa Phillip Randolph, Whitney Young, and Bayard Rustin, who were indispensable members of the movement.[18] The history of the Black church, from the Pietist and Methodist movements to the Jim Crow era, the Civil Rights Movement, and the outgrowth of the Azusa Street Revival, sets the framework for understanding how a culture was established that concentrated power in male leadership, which reinforced IPV and underreporting. The European immigrants that migrated to America to escape the abuse, power, and control of the Church of England utilized the same weapons they fled from to subjugate women and persons of color.

Further, Blacks that were enslaved fought for freedom from prejudice, oppression, abuse, power, and control against the White male power structure more than likely adopted the same tactics to subjugate Black women, continuing the male cultural tradition of the submission and oppression of women. Whether this is indicative of the culture of the times or not, the Black church implemented the same culture of subjugation and oppression of women as victims of the culture and framework instituted by the dominant culture. Furthermore, the history of the Black church displays an organization attempting to escape the power struggle against White America, oppressive government, politicians, and federal and state legislatures that sponsored oppression by using the Scriptures to subjugate them into obedience by attacking their self-esteem and self-confidence, instilling fear, and initiating punishment and retaliation to maintain power and control. The cultural tradition of male dominance that begins in the slave era, continuing through the Jim Crow era and the Civil Rights Movement, serves as the substratum for male dominance in the Black church, support for IPV, and discouragement of reporting. The cultural tradition of White male dominance that Black leaders worked so diligently to overcome became transmitted into the structure and administration of ministry culture.

17. Green, *Voices in Black Political Thought*, 1–15.
18. Robinson, *Black Movements in America*, 139–49.

The mindset of males during the eras of slavery, Jim Crow, and the Civil Rights Movement is crucial in understanding male dominance and the subjugation of women. Although Blacks were enslaved, males in the community held the same gender-biased beliefs as White males regarding the status of women and their position in society. The belief system regarding women and their position in society produced an atmosphere for the acceptance of abuse and continued subjugation to male dominance.

The Culture of the Black Church in America

Understanding the culture of the Black church helps us to understand the underpinnings for the development of the system of power utilized to support abuse and control against women. The historical characteristics of the Black church in America provide the framework for understanding the concentration of power and control in the pulpit. The culture of the Black church is vast and runs deep with unwritten rules established over the course of hundreds of years and a cultivated code of secrecy that forced women to remain silent about IPV and never report.

Culture can be defined as the philosophical beliefs, customs, thought processes, methodology, behaviors, and way of life for a group of individuals, a place, or an organization.[19] The Black church has developed and adopted a culture based upon a historical framework deeply rooted in African traditions and customs. For example, the church has a strong sense of culture, community, and family that extends to singles in the congregation. There is a sense of no one left behind and no one left out, especially during holidays and special occasions where community and family gather together. The sense of belonging is crucial to the culture of the congregation coupled in identification with a family name.

The family name, in most cases, was all that Blacks held in their possession, especially during slavery. Everything was in the name: life, hope, and, more importantly, a sense of knowing your cultural heritage, which gave a person identity in the community. The church was the central location where families gathered together and supported one another in times of need.

The community pooled their resources together to ensure that no one in the community lacked basic necessities. This established a community culture in which a village existed for the safety and protection of its

19. Lawson and Garrod, *Dictionary of Sociology*, 56.

members as well as fellowship and encouragement. The culture of community is valuable regarding fellowship with the saints, whether it's joining another church for worship, sharing a meal with members after church, youth and singles hanging out having fun, married couples vacationing together, or the mothers' board having a prayer meeting. To be in community was essential for the survival of the church, especially during slavery, Jim Crow, and the Civil Rights Movement; fellowship was critical in providing comfort, edification, and encouragement for individuals who endured suffering, trials, hardships, and tribulations.

The culture of the congregation is grounded in the notions of community and fellowship, but also food. The idea of great-tasting food is a staple in Black church culture and most everything happens around the table with a meal. Black congregational culture utilizes food as an invitation for people to participate in community. Food items such as collard greens, fried chicken, fried catfish, hush puppies, cornbread, yams, peach cobbler, and sweet potato pies are just a few dishes served up when the saints gather together for fellowship.[20] The church is also deeply grounded in spiritual roots that have shaped the culture, traditions, norms, and customs that permeate the atmosphere of the Black church today. Black church culture in America has roots in the West African culture of the Gullahs, the first slaves to arrive by ship in the Carolinas. The Gullahs came to America with deep spiritual roots, grounded in centuries of African nostalgia with dancing, singing, and heavy drum bass music.[21]

The theological foundation and beliefs that formed the culture of the Black church in times past remain intact, especially the issue of male dominance and female submission. The church continues to manifest a culture in which control is utilized by pastors to set the stage for how the church grows, develops, and evolves.[22] The spiritual culture of parishioners is also entrenched in strict obedience to God, obedience to church leadership, order, and full support of the pastor and ministry. This culture of obedience to the pastor and church leadership has set the stage for the acceptance and tolerance of IPV against women.

The defined gender roles have contributed to the oppression of women as they experience the pressure of fulfilling those roles to be perceived as godly wives worthy of honor and acceptance. Although times have changed

---

20. Battle, *Black Church in America*, 45.
21. Joyner, "'Believer I Know.'"
22. Lincoln, *Black Church in the African American Experience*, 76–91.

within the Black family, with more single mothers as head of the household, in marriage, Black men continue to dominate the family structure. Furthermore, the role of Black women in church has remained consistent for the last five decades, even though women continue to experience more freedom and serve in leadership positions such as pastor and bishop. In the COGIC, Baptist denominations, and conservative organizations, most women have no propensity to enter into leadership positions they believe should be held by men. Although Black women in other denominations may have no desire to serve in the position of pastor, most are content with fulfilling traditional female roles in the church.

The concept and roles of marriage and family play an essential role in understanding IPV, power, and control. Although roles within marriage and families have changed over time with the addition of higher income, livability, and socioeconomic status, most Black married couples follow traditional roles in marriage and family. The roles listed above are ingrained in the history and structure of Black culture embedded within the family and church life.

The Role of Black Males

The role of Black men has its genesis in the traditions and customs of African history, with the male positioned as patriarch of the family and head of household. Males are groomed for this role during their early teenage years and trained accordingly to provide leadership for their families, especially at the demise of the family patriarch.[23] Black males are inculcated with lessons in leadership and talks with fathers who help them understand the importance of leading the family in the father's absence. Although the traditional Black family has experienced a decline due to a lack of fathers in the home,[24] most families acknowledge males as the leader of the family, especially in the Southern, Bible Belt states.[25] Black males are perceived as leaders in at least four roles of family life: *head of the household, leader of the family, protector of the family,* and *provider for the family.* The church reinforces these leadership roles through the use of Scriptures to support the subjugation of women.

---

23. Mitchell, *African American Fatherhood*, 37–46.
24. Tucker and James, "New Families, New Functions," 94–95.
25. Ibid.

Furthermore, leadership roles and structure are articulated even when congregants come from fatherless households and experience conversion; they are acclimated to the family structure with the male as head of the household as well as provider, leader, and protector of the family.

Head of the Household

The title "head of the household" is one of great appellations bestowed upon the Black male; it is a sign of respect in the family and community. Head of the household is a term designated for males alone, although females take on the role in the absence of males in the home.[26] Being the head of the house comes with certain amenities earned based upon leadership and natural selection as the patriarch of the family, such as being the first person to eat at the dinner table, leading the family in prayer, and acting as family spokesperson and the decisive voice in all family business and financial matters. This is inclusive of how much money is allotted for mortgage payments, car payments, and activities, as well as decisions about when to relocate, including moving out of state. Although more Black families are embracing alternative forms of marriage such as swinging and egalitarian, as well as abandoning altogether the traditional family with the male as head of household, the majority of Black families continue to embrace the traditional style of family leadership with the male as head of the household.

Provider for the Family

Black males are also the main provider of all needs for the family, whether financial, emotional, or spiritual. Black males are trained to ensure that food is on the table, the family is clothed, transportation is ready, and the family has a roof over their heads.[27] Although the role of provider has changed with more women entering the workforce and more fathers staying at home to care for the children,[28] the role of provider is reserved for the male in the Black family. The Black church leans heavily on 1 Timothy 5:8, which states that "if any fails to provide for his own, he is worse than an infidel or

---

26. Hill, *Black Intimacies*, 51–58.
27. McAdoo, "Roles of African American Fathers," 183–90.
28. Franklin, "African American Families," 5–9.

unbeliever" (KJV). Black males pride themselves on the ability to fully care for their families and ensure all basic family needs are met.

Further black males will sacrifice their own needs to meet the needs of their families. They understand the need to ensure that when basic necessities such as food are lacking in the household, they are the first to offer up their own meal to allow their wife and children to eat and be full, while they accept less. Further, Black males will starve rather than be viewed in the church and community as an infidel, one who thinks of himself first in lieu of placing the needs of the entire family above his title of head of household, provider, and leader. The goal here is to paint an image to the outside world of a strong Black male who provides for the family in order to cover up narcissistic behaviors in which they abuse, control, and subjugate their wives.

Leader of the Family

The next important role that Black males fulfill in the family dynamic is that of the leader. Leadership is defined as having influence[29] and males are inculcated with the concept of leading the family, church, and community from an early age. This notion of leadership has its origin in the lineage of African history that has produced kings, queens, princes, princesses, military generals, and many other great leaders. Although Black males were reduced to the position of slaves and three fifths of a person upon coming to America, they continued to function as valiant and respected leaders in their communities, even among White slave masters.[30] The role of the Black male is to lead with dignity, respect, integrity, and, at times, a stern hand and a deep voice, walking tall, proud of the God-given responsibility to lead the family in the commandments of the Lord.

The wife and children look to the male for trust and leadership as he leads with vision and purpose as the cornerstone of the family. This title of leader comes with the designation of decision maker in family business, consultant for all family members, strong influencer on marriage for their sons and daughters, and highest authority in all family matters. The title of leader means they lead and everyone else follows, and the church continues to reinforce this message in their teachings on roles in the family. These God-given responsibilities cannot be fulfilled by the female; for a woman

29. Maxwell, *Developing the Leader within You*, 1.
30. McAdoo and McAdoo, *Dynamics of African American Fathers*, 3–9.

to assume this role in the presence of Black males in the home is taboo and disdained by the church.

Protector of the Family

The Black male serves as the chief protector of the family, which is an important role especially for his wife and daughters. He is trained to employ every possible tactic in order to protect his family from dangers in the neighborhood, schoolyard, church, and broader community. The Jim Crow era and struggle for civil rights highlighted the need for males to protect their families by any means necessary against prejudice, bigotry, and racism.[31] The family is left vulnerable and open for attack from strangers and intruders if Black men fail to provide security to their families. The Black family suffered a great loss when males were publicly whipped, executed, and sold to slave masters, thus breaking down the traditional family structure. The rise of drugs and gang violence swept through the inner cities of America, thus reemphasizing the need for males to ensure their families were protected from the ills of society. The role of protector is one that is taken seriously in the community and it is an important part of leadership for males. Black men are trained from an early age to become protectors of the family, church, and community.

The Role of Males in the Black Church

The role of the Black male in the church environment is very similar to that of the family context. The males occupy nearly all the top echelon leadership positions in the church. As previously stated, although women are beginning to enter into top leadership positions of the church, the balance still heavily favors males. Most leadership and financial decisions are made by males in the church while women are relegated to menial tasks in the kitchen, nursery, and Sunday school, or perhaps assisting with basic financial matters such as counting offerings after service.[32] Black males in church leadership continue to exhibit ultimate authority in the church, following in the cultural tradition previously mentioned regarding dominance and

---

31. Johnson and Staples, *Black Families at the Crossroads*, 155–64.
32. Ibid.

the subjugation of women based upon their own interpretation of scriptural texts.

The role of males in the church is to lead their families and ensure that all members adhere to their leadership to avoid embarrassment and show their ability to control their family. Black males in the church environment, especially elders and deacons, pride themselves on possessing complete dominance over their children, oftentimes citing 1 Timothy 5:18, which poses the question, "How can one rule the house of God, if they cannot rule in their own houses?" This became and remains the gold standard for males in the church, especially those who desire to enter into the ministerial work of pastoring. The idea is that strong Black males are needed to shoulder the burden of building great ministries; however, the role of strength has been transformed and has become synonymous with abuse, power, control, and the subjugation of women. The subjugation of women remains an immense problem in the church, continuing in the tradition of the male culture of dominance, power, and control acquired from the heritage, traditions, cultures, and norms of Africa combined with the European mindset and attitude towards women.

The Role of the Pastor

The Black church has a long-standing history of demonstrating a high level of respect for the senior pastor of the ministry. They give him high esteem and deference, placing the lives of their families in the hands of the pastor, whom they emphatically believe has been chosen by God to lead them to the land of promise. Black families seek spiritual guidance, direction, counsel, and prayer from the pastor, as well as home and hospital visits, teaching, and preaching that will lift up their souls after experiencing suffering and other issues faced during the week between church services. Most Black families trust that the pastor will assist in their family's decision-making process, as they believe the pastor has a special connection with God and will lead the family in the right direction.[33] The pastor yields great authority in the church, with most congregants accepting the word of the pastor as gospel. The family is taught to never question the authority of the pastor under any circumstance; to do this could be perceived as sin.

The pastor is almost never referred to by his first name; instead, he is referred to by either the initials of his first and middle name and his full

---

33. Taylor, Chatters, and Levin, *Religion in the Lives of African Americans*, 111–36.

last name, or simply by the title of pastor and his last name. Although more Black pastors are comfortable with being called Pastor John or Pastor Bob, the ecclesiastical title always precedes the name. This has great implications for the role of women in the family and the church setting. The respect given to pastors in Black churches is imperative in understanding the lack of reporting by victims and congregants who abide in subjugated roles with little to no authority in decision making.

The pastor is the center of attention and attraction as the congregation seeks guidance and direction in their daily lives, clinging to every word spoken as a newborn baby clings to its mother.[34] The pastor is responsible for the spiritual direction and formation of the entire congregation and this has great significance in terms of culture. The pastor determines what messages are taught, which sermons are preached, and how information is disseminated from the pulpit and all areas of the church. For example, IPV is considered a family issue, a legal and criminal issue, but also a spiritual issue that can have direct impact on the culture of the congregation in terms of how abuse is perceived and addressed. The topic of domestic violence can only become part of the culture contingent upon the pastor's willingness to discuss the issue transparently and fully support efforts to increase awareness and education. The spiritual culture of the church has protected the issue of abuse and control under the umbrella of secrecy and silence.

The issue is hidden to stifle discussion and divert the attention of parishioners away from policy and programs that serve to educate and train Christians about domestic violence and equip them with the skill set to provide assistance. The secrecy and silence surrounding abuse, coupled with control by male leadership, allow family violence to remain veiled under the guise of spirituality and inhibits the issue from being exposed in its true nature and form. The pastor in the Black church plays a critical role in the church for the dissemination of information and must refrain from utilizing codified language when speaking to the congregation, small groups, or one on one about IPV. Pastors set the tone and direction on how information is reported and to whom the information is reported.

In addition to this, males sit in other powerful positions such as associate minister, elder, deacon, board member, trustee member, and administrator, which carry great weight and influence in all church-related matters. Although more women are fulfilling key leadership roles in the

---

34. Ibid., 11–13.

Black church, the male voice still dominates almost all final decisions related to the church, business, and ministry.

The Role of the Black Female in the Family

The role of the Black female in the family setting is one of submission to the role of the Black male. The history of the female role also has its genesis in the African traditions, norms, heritage, and customs. The role of the female is that of the family succor, providing care and nourishment to her husband and children. The Black female is the primary caregiver for the family, especially for the children, who run into the arms of their mother when they skin their knees after a fall on the playground as well as when more serious issues arise, such as dating and marriage.[35]

The female is viewed as more understanding and approachable as compared to males, who tend to perceive issues from a logical perspective with no emotional attachment. Black females exhibit a certain level of leadership in the family concentrated in the areas of emotional support and active listening to issues and concerns. Females who have built a level of trust based upon their wisdom and ability to induce their husbands during pillow talk are given an expanded role of leadership within the family, especially when the husband is absent from the home during work.[36]

Their level of authority in the area of discipline is strongly supported by the males, who make it extremely clear that no disrespect by children against their mothers will be tolerated. Black females are second in command in the leadership structure of the family, having the authority to direct and guide the family with a big stick, and in some cases upsetting the woman is worse than upsetting the man.

The Role of the Black Female in Church

The role of the Black female in the church is similar to her role in the home and family as succor, listener, and nurturer. Although females in the Black Pentecostal church are rising to positions of preacher, minister, associate pastor, and senior pastor, females continue to serve primarily in subservient positions such as secretary, administrative assistant, kitchen administrator,

---

35. Dixon, *African American Relationships*, 69.
36. Gilkes, *If It Wasn't for the Woman*, 76–90.

nurse, and usher.[37] Black females still do not have the same level of authority or voice at the table as compared to Black males. For example, many women pastors who are married still provide the primary level of care and household responsibilities such as cooking, cleaning, and washing and drying clothes.

The domestic duties of the Black female in the family do not necessarily cease just because they perform ecclesiastical duties. The women's department is led by a woman who is respected as the leader of women but has limited influence in the church beyond that role. The issues that impact women are primarily discussed in women's meetings among women who gather at a specified date and time. Black women rarely serve on the important boards of the church, namely the board of directors or board of trustees, and if they are selected to serve in that capacity their influence is overshadowed by the presence of males.

The education level of females plays a vital role with regard to how they are utilized in the broader aspect of ministry. For example, if a female has a certain education level, such as a master's degree or doctorate, she is called upon to function as a consultant to the project and may even be asked to serve on the board in the event it is a win-win for the ministry and perhaps connects the church with valuable resources to increase its status and position.

In most cases, men who do not have the same degree of education as women continue to serve in the most important positions of the church as compared to women with more education. Although women played a vital role in traditional African societies in positions such as priestess, their role in the Black church, as a result of Western Christianity, changed significantly as the Baptists and Methodists adopted the European paradigm of Christianity.[38] The church mother holds a very powerful position in the church and exhibits great influence among women congregants.

They are revered as saintly women and establish relationships of trust and confidence, oftentimes serving as the confidant to many women in the church. Although the church mother has a key position in the church, their voices remain limited to that of the pastor and male leadership. However, the voice of the church mother can greatly assist in awareness and education about abuse, and serve as a great asset in the effort to assist women in addressing IPV issues. Although church mothers can have influence in

37. Ibid.
38. Whelcher, *History and Heritage of African American Churches*, 115–20.

addressing domestic violence issues, they must be careful not to act as mediators to protect the pastor, male leadership, and abusers.

Traditional male and female roles in the home, family life, and church still function hierarchically, particularly in Black marriages. Leon Podles suggests that femininity can have a negative impact on masculinity. He states that young boys achieve masculinity only when they reject females; his quest for manhood begins with a break from his mother. Podles further suggests that in order for a male to love any woman, he must first discard his mother or suffer the consequence of never becoming masculine.

Embracing masculinity by driving the "female" out of themselves is the genesis of the mindset in which males perceive females in a lower position in the community and family.[39] However, Ron Clark states that instead of breaking with females to *achieve* masculinity, the notion of masculinity is destroyed by removing the "female" from the lives of males. Masculinity is abolished when males fail to understand how to interact with females and embrace healthy relationships.[40] This is imperative for the Black church and Christendom to understand in order to end family violence and the subjugation of women in the church.

Marriage in the Black Culture

In the Black church, especially in the Southern states, there is a time-honored understanding of the biblical view of marriage and family, where the notion of marriage as existing only between one man and one woman remains strong in the twenty-first century.[41]

Although more Blacks are embracing non-traditional forms of marriage such as open marriages and polyamory, most still favor the traditional form of marriage between a man and woman.[42] The early antebellum years in American history did not afford Blacks the same rights as Whites and laws prohibited them from marrying in the same manner. Blacks could not enter into civil contracts such as marriage and thus were innovative in the art of wedding ceremonies.

Blacks created wedding ceremonies such as jumping the broom, Scripture weddings, and wedding banquets for the entire community to

---

39. Podles, *Church Impotent*, 38–41.
40. Clark, *Am I Sleeping with the Enemy?*, 49–52.
41. Belgrave and Allison, *African American Psychology*, 230.
42. Stanford, *Homophobia in the Black Church*, 142–44.

celebrate as they were prohibited to marry legally until after emancipation. They now experience the same positivity in marriage as other ethnicities.[43] Black church culture has an expectation that their children enter in holy matrimony and embrace the institution of marriage. The Black community believes in the notion of traditional marriage that served as the foundation of society in African culture and tradition of family. The notion of marriage in the Black church and community is still perceived as important part of family culture[44] and established on the great traditions of African culture and customs; the Black church strongly believes that marriage fosters strong families.

Conclusion

The historical aspect of the Black church is helpful in understanding the continuation of domestic violence and the subjugation of women. The church has continued in the traditions of its African heritage, customs, norms, and adopting the cultural mindset and attitude against women of European males during the era of slavery.

The Black congregation, specifically males in leadership positions, upheld and supported the subjugation of women and encouraged females to fulfill a specific role of submission that mostly continues today. Although more and more women are challenging the traditional role of women in the family, church setting, and redefining the nature of that role, they continue to remain in a subservient position to men in the church and family.

This profoundly impacts the issue of domestic abuse against women and underreporting, especially when women are not in positions of power or influence to contribute to the discussion of how IPV is addressed within the congregation.

The position and role of the pastor is critical in moving issues of abuse to the forefront and ensuring that women are protected and have a vehicle for reporting. The voice and influence of the pastor must change the course of how domestic violence is addressed by taking a public stand against the issue from behind the pulpit and articulating a message that brings awareness, education, and training to the church; sending a clear signal that male dominance and submission of females is disdained; and encouraging women and congregants to report abuse to law enforcement or church officials.

43. Scafidi, *Who Owns Culture?*, 38–39.
44. Foster, *'Til Death or Distance Do Us Part*, 103–4.

Prophetic voices must rise from within the church to ignite a discussion of the oppression of women and abuse.

The church must teach males how to love their neighbors and wives as they love themselves, and teach that to love God means they love their wives. This is one method and a first step to significantly reduce IPV in the Black church and discontinue the practice of protecting abusers, re-victimizing women, and concealing the issue from the congregation.

The church must be educated about domestic violence in order to help women report it and the church must present options in the event a woman desires to escape abuse. Pastors in the Black church must be aware that males have the ability to underfunction in marriage and relationships by overcompensating in the roles of provider, protector, and head of household while using these roles as a cover to overfunction by continuing abuse against women.

Chapter 3

The Theological Foundations that Support IPV in the Black Church

THE BLACK CHURCH EMBRACES a long tradition of theological engagement and framework for the application of Scripture directly related to relationships, specifically marriage between husbands and wives. The church relies heavily upon the Bible as the definitive text to outline the nature of interaction between married couples, parents and children, and pastors and parishioners. The Scriptures are immensely important to Christians, who utilize the sacred text as the supreme authority in all church and relationship matters. Most congregations resolve disputes with the support of biblical interpretation, with the pastor as the judge in the black robe, gavel in hand, utilizing the pulpit as his ruling bench.

Theology, in its most basic definition, means the study of God's nature, essence, character, attributes, and interaction with creation.[1] The study of God is inclusive of how we encounter and envision faith in our daily lives as we seek to live out that faith in a pragmatic manner. For example, when there is a death in the family, in the family, individuals contemplate all aspects of death and how it impacts their lives, wondering how God will see them through. When there is tragedy in the world like that experienced with Hurricane Katrina, the typhoon that obliterated the Philippines, the Ebola virus in West Africa, the riots in Ferguson, Missouri, and New York City, and the beheading of an American journalist, we deliberate about the immanence and transcendence of God in the affairs of mankind.[2] Early church fathers such as Clement, Athanasius, Cyprian, Tertullian, and Augustine not only

---

1. Harris, *Christian Theology*, 1–2.
2. Placher, *Why Bother with Theology?*, 1.

The Theological Foundations that Support IPV

made invaluable contributions to the early church, but set the stage for theology today.

The theological foundation and framework of the Black church has its origins in the Protestant Reformation, the Methodist movement, the Azusa Street Revival, and Black preachers in the antebellum period that promulgated the message of freedom and liberation from the cruel oppression of slavery. This became the rallying cry of the Black church and attracted the attention of slaves from the far corners of the country. Distinguished theologian and scholar James Cone introduced Christendom to the concept of Black Theology to depict a God on the side of the oppressed and marginalized. Black Theology has a strong emphasis on biblical texts that address freedom, oppression, and social justice, which has become the battle cry for the Black church and other oppressed groups.[3]

The holiness movement produced a theological foundation of sanctification and baptism of the Holy Spirit with the evidence of speaking in tongues. The theological foundation of the holiness movement focused primarily on strict obedience, living a separated life from the world, adherence to prayer, fasting, Bible study, and fellowship. The holiness movement embraces Christology, pneumatology, and eschatology, with a strong emphasis on soteriology. The rich theological foundation of the church has undergone a transformation in the understanding and interpretation of marriage and relationships. Although Christians place great emphasis on the Bible, the theological foundation has suffered tremendously in the arena of proper analysis. The sermons of freedom and deliverance quickly turned into sermons of hell, brimstone, and fire from the pulpit.

The theology of the church that pertains to male leadership and marriage supported the established culture of male dominance, oppression, and subjugation of women that established the unwritten protocol for abuse, power, and control. The task in this section is to discover the methodology utilized by pastors to subdue women and fortify the prison of oppression with males as the wardens. Previously, the link was established between abuse in the Black church and the adoption of male cultural dominance and submission of women from their heritage in some African traditions and the customs of the European structure during slavery. The theological foundation of the church utilized to oppress women continues in the church today in most mainstream denominations. The Scripture we will

---

3. Cone, *God of the Oppressed*, 163–83.

examine will expand our comprehension of how certain passages were interpreted by pastors and explicated to congregants.

Education

During the slavery, Jim Crow, and Civil Rights eras, Blacks in many instances were denied the opportunity to obtain quality education. Instead, they formed segregated schools to assist with educational achievement.[4] Blacks who were one generation removed from slavery and could not read or write depended upon their children to read and interpret writing as well as sign documents for their parents.[5] The lack of education also extended to the Black church, as most individuals had no formal education, even lacking basic reading and writing skills.

The lack of reading and writing comprehension continued to be passed down to future generations and congregants, who could not properly decipher the Old and New Testaments in the original Hebrew and Greek context. Christians sat in the pews faithfully for each service, patiently waiting for the pastor to deliver a fiery sermon. The congregation depended solely upon the pastor, deacon, or missionary to expound on the Scriptures and assist in helping parishioners apply God's word to their daily lives. This is an essential aspect of the establishment of the theological foundation in the Black church as congregants had limited institutions to receive understanding of the Bible. Although congregants built a relationship with God, there was virtually no opportunity to comprehend the Bible in context. Pastors also experienced immense difficulty with reading and writing comprehension as well as issues with articulation, enunciation, and an overall command of the English vernacular. Congregants, who leaned so heavily on the pastor, were in most cases unaware that he encountered the same literacy and writing issues. Although some pastors obtained education, including doctorate degrees, the great majority of pastors were at the same educational level as the members. This caused grave issues with providing correct exegesis of Scripture.[6]

For example, pastors propagated that women should not wear pants, using Deuteronomy 22:5 (KJV) as the foundation for theological exegesis. They literally believed that the passage, written in 40 B.C., meant that God

---

4. Chafe, Gavins, and Korstad, *Remembering Jim Crow*, 152–55.
5. Belt-Beyan, *Emergence of African American Literacy Traditions*, 79–88.
6. Lummis, "Heart and Head in Reaching Pastors of Black Churches."

prohibited women from wearing pants in the same fashion as males. Although these exegetical issues were paramount in the holiness/Pentecostal church, the same issues existed in fundamentalist churches as well.

The issues with literacy and writing significantly impacted the ability of the church and pastors to properly exegete Scripture in a manner consistent with the transliteration of the Bible. In addition to this, misinformation was transmitted to congregants, who then shared the same misinformation to the broader community. Thus, the information continually changed and adapted to various audiences, readers, and speakers. Congregants were encouraged to wholly trust the word of the pastor and never question his authority no matter how limited his research, study, and reading and writing skill set.

Congregants were taught to accept spirituality and the moving of the Spirit as a sign of God's approval in lieu of correct interpretations of the Bible. Thus, the theological framework was established in the Black church on an unstable substratum that would become the hallmark of church experience and lay the cornerstone for the support and continuation of abuse, power, oppression, control, and subjugation of women. Education in the Black church followed the same dictates as in biblical times, when a few educated elites held power over the uneducated masses, thus utilizing education as a means to control and subjugate women.

This section will primarily focus on the theology and interpretation of Scripture utilized by the Black church to define the roles of husband and wife. This is imperative in aiding us to understand the underpinnings for abuse and control of women as well as the origin of how power and control is obtained by pastors and males to keep women in submission and discourage them from reporting. This section will also examine several passages in the Old and New Testaments utilized by pastors in sermons and teachings that provide support for abuse against women.

Although more and more males are victims of abuse, the overwhelming majority of victims are women abused at the hands of men.[7] The texts that we will examine are as follows: Genesis 2:19, 21–15; 3:16; Numbers 30:5; Deuteronomy 24:1–5; Proverbs 19:13; 21:9; 25:24; 27:15; 31:10–31; Matthew 19:1–9; Mark 10:1–12; Galatians 3:28; 1 Corinthians 7:1–17; 11:1–12; Ephesians 5:21–32; Colossians 3:18–19; 1 Timothy 2:9–15; 3:4–5, and 1 Peter 3:1–9.

---

7. McCue, *Domestic Violence* (2008), 77–79.

The Old Testament

Genesis

The book of Genesis outlines four major theological themes that are helpful in understanding the writing: (1) God as creator; (2) the entrance of sin into the created order, which alters the original created order; (3) God's judgment upon humankind; and (4) God's preservation of humankind through unmerited favor and grace.[8] The main themes of Genesis will help provide a clear understanding of the book from the origin of life to the creation of humanity, the sin and disobedience of Adam, the fall, and the introduction to monotheism.

A theology of the book of Genesis is important in understanding the trajectory for the theology of the church with regard to marriage, and is inclusive of the interpretation of Scripture to control and keep women in a position of submission to male authority by utilizing Genesis 3:16. We will examine preceding texts in Genesis 2 to set the background for chapter 3. The passage beginning in 2:19 provides context into the mind of God preceding the creation of Adam and Eve. God created all things for man in the first five days of creation and called his creation "good," but when he created man on the sixth day he called the creation "very good."

The writer then recounts the instructions given to Adam regarding the tree of the knowledge of good and evil in the midst of the garden. The writer reveals additional insight into the thought of God, who observes that Adam is alone and states that it is not good for him to be alone. God shifts from the aloneness of Adam and re-enters creation by forming the wild animals and birds of the sky, giving Adam the task to name them. The story shifts back to Adam, with God removing a rib from his side and forming his mate from that rib. God brings her to Adam, who names her "woman." Adam took her as bone of his bone and flesh of his flesh and they were naked and not ashamed.

The phrase "not ashamed" is imperative to understand marriage before the fall. I believe that it was always God's intent for women (as well as men) not to be ashamed regarding marriage. Next, the text focuses on the fall of humankind via disobedience of the instructions concerning the tree of the knowledge of good and evil. After Adam eats from the tree, God looks for him and discovers that he is covered in leaves and questions Adam concerning why he is covered in leaves. God then pronounces judgment on

8. Bergant, *Genesis*, 3–8.

humankind and brings sweat upon the forehead of Adam while also cursing the ground. The punishment for Eve is pain in child birth; her desire would be for her husband who would rule over her. The Black church captures the story of the fall as the primary focal point of a theology of marriage, specifically the hierarchical structure of relationship between a husband and wife. The Black church places great emphasis on the word "rule," which carries the meaning of having dominion and authority over, but more importantly means to lead, protect, and guard; which is accomplished by giving proper respect to all household members.[9]

James McKeown states that prior to the fall, Adam and Eve likely lived in harmony and the term "rule" was implemented as a consequence of sin and utilized after the fall and as a result of turpitude.[10] Pastors continue to struggle with properly exegeting 3:16, which has led to the development of their misinterpretation of the passage and subjugation of women. Pastors must be encouraged to exegete the word "rule" to mean "lead in the context of marriage and God's relationship with the church." Although God rules over the church, his methodology in ruling is to lead the church with love, compassion, and grace guiding the church through the Holy Spirit, with Jesus as the head. As God leads his church with patience and mercy, he does not abuse his church. The theology of marriage in the Black church should mirror the relationship between God and his bride, the church, in which husbands lead and carry the relationship by initiating love, care, and compassion in the same manner Yahweh interacts with his bride, the church.

Numbers 30:1–5

A major theme of the book of Numbers centers on the presence of God among his people. The Lord made his presence known in the midst of Israel, revealing himself as a cloud by day and pillar of fire by night. When the cloud moved, the camp of Israel moved, and when the cloud settled, Israel settled. The presence of the Lord also provided providence in the wilderness, feeding Israel with manna from heaven and quails when their palate could no longer bear bread.[11]

The book of Numbers offers the reader an understanding of God's patience with Israel; they wandered in the wilderness forty years for

---

9. Schuetze, *1 Timothy, 2 Timothy, Titus*, 47–54.
10. McKeown, *Genesis*, 36–38.
11. Goldingay, *Numbers and Deuteronomy for Everyone*, 6–9.

disobedience and idolatry, yet God was patient and not willing that any should perish.[12]

Although Numbers 30:1–5 discusses the relationship between fathers and daughters and women and husbands, the passage provides insight into the notions of power and oppression in the family against women and in the Black church. The Black church has utilized this text of Scripture to exert authority over women's lives, which has led to abuse and oppression of women in the church. Numbers 30:1–5 emphasizes the role of the father in the private and public affairs of daughters. Women residing in traditional Jewish culture had no legal rights; they were to be in subjection to their husbands. In 30:1–5, Moses gives instructions to fathers concerning the vows of daughters. When a daughter who is unmarried makes a vow and the father holds his peace, then the vow stands. However, when the father hears the vow from his daughter's lips and disagrees with the vow, then the vow does not stand. The term for "vow" in the Hebrew, *neder*, refers to an oath or promise made by an individual concerning something in their heart that they desire to do or fulfill.[13] The same method for approving or disapproving vows with a married woman was conducted in the same manner between a father and daughter.

During early times in Jewish history, in the absence of legal documents, the word of an individual meant everything and a person was bound to their word.[14] The act of the husband or father approving or disapproving the vow made by a daughter or wife has been mistranslated by the Black church (as well as some White conservative churches) to mean that husbands and fathers have complete authority over their wives and daughters.

Calum Carmichael helps us understand the nature of the text in which the father or husband approves or disapproves of a vow made by a daughter or wife. He states that approving and disapproving of a vow suggests that the action is being conducted out of love for the female and her respect for the wisdom of her father or husband by using the example of Jacob and Rachel.[15] Further, the text does not imply that the father or husband governs the thoughts of the female, but suggests that since God is love and the Holy Spirit leads and guides us into all truth, so fathers and husbands must act

---

12. Stubbs, *Numbers*, 29–33.
13. Ashley, *Book of Numbers*, 574.
14. Nowell, *Numbers*, 126–27.
15. Carmichael, *Book of Numbers*, 149–50.

in the same nature and love of God in the best interest of the female.[16] This is an act of protection for females, a covering and shield to prevent danger and trouble, helping females count up the costs when making a vow and not putting their hands to the gospel plow and reflecting back. Men were encouraged to attain the utmost level of integrity and ethics when selecting a suitable mate for their daughters, thus the onus was placed on the males (not females) to protect their daughters during such a serious time in their lives as they prepared for and embraced marriage.[17] The church must abandon its literal interpretation of the passage in the sense of authority and control, particularly for fathers, who have the responsibility of raising and training daughters.

Christians must view the passage through the lens of love, compassion, and leadership, as well as protection for females. This is equally important for young females, who at times sense the necessity to participate in life activities that are not necessarily beneficial or do not promote healthy lifestyle choices. The intent is to encourage a conversation and explanation in lieu of directives and orders in an effort to maintain the relationship in love and grace. Pastors should encourage parents to understand their children and lead them with love, respect, and protection rather than "putting women in their place." The pulpit can be a powerful weapon in the Black church, from which the pastor has the obligation to change the nature of the message to fathers and husbands to emanate the love and compassion of God through servant leadership. When the message from the pastor is presented and understood in the context of dominance and control, this erects the foundation for the entrance for IPV against women in the church.

Proverbs

The writing in the book of Proverbs will help our comprehension of the scriptures utilized to continue the power structure of abuse, control, dominance, and subjugation of women in the Black church. There are four texts in Proverbs—19:13; 21:9 and 25:24; 27:15; 31:10–31—that have been utilized to keep women in a subservient position in the church, the home, and society. These passages have helped to shape a negative image of women in the eyes of males while helping to establish a cultural attitude of men towards women that reduces women to an inferior status. The terms

---

16. Brown, *Message of Numbers*, 262–65.
17. Ibid.

"contentious" and "brawling" characterize women as arduous, unable to build rapport or establish effective marital relationships.

Proverbs 19:13

Proverbs 19:13 utilizes the term "contentious" to depict women and compares this type of woman to a continual dripping. The comparison of a wife to a continual drip paints a vivid picture of a woman who lacks self-control and is unable to refrain from nagging and contentious conduct.[18] This depiction gives life to the current stereotypes of women in film and journalism today. The writer of Proverbs also pens in 27:13 an almost identical verse to 19:13, comparing a contentious woman to a continual dropping on a rainy day; the writer states that nagging and contentious women are one and the same.[19]

The weather in Oregon is rainy and at times drenches individuals as they enjoy the "liquid sunshine." The rain continues for days on end, transitioning from sprinkle to shower, to rain, to downpour. The picture concerning rain in Oregon compared to a contentious woman, in my opinion, further denigrates women to the lowest level of humanity, almost in comparison to an animal, which lacks self-control. The Black church has utilized these passages to control the behavior and, more importantly, the expression of women, coercing them into the position of a docile newborn needing the assistance of a parent to help control her actions. Further, church mothers and women group leaders, who yield power and influence in the Black church, also present these passages of Scripture to assist in the submission of women without understanding how their actions support male dominance in the church.

Proverbs 21:9 and 25:24

Proverbs 21:9 and 25:24 portray women in a damaging perspective and perceive them as second-class citizens to the male power structure. The passages are identical and the writer suggests that it is better to dwell in the corner of the housetop than with a brawling woman in a wide house.[20] Most

18. Longman, *Proverbs*, 369.
19. Fox, *Proverbs 10–31*, 810.
20. Horne, *Proverbs-Ecclesiastes*, 259–60.

scholars agree that during biblical times there were probably no "corners" on the rooftop, but McKane suggests that these were open-air spaces, so that the verse carries the meaning that it is better to be exposed to outside elements than in a house with a brawling woman.[21] The corner of the housetop proposes a place of hiding from a woman who engages in fights and skirmishes. The writer does not state explicitly who should flee to the corner of the housetop; however, it should be implicitly understood that the writer is referring to a husband in relationship with his wife. Furthermore, the writer identifies the house in question as a wide house, meaning there is a lot of space and room, perhaps for a woman to engage in combat comfortably without interference from furniture or household items. The women in both passages are depicted as fighters and both present women as individuals who lack self-restraint, unable to resolve issues without violence.

When viewed in isolation, these passages describe women as the aggressors, instigators, abusers, and controllers. This intriguing exposé gives the appearance that men are the victims of abuse and need protection from women. The Black church utilizes these passages of Scripture to continue the suppression of women in the church by emphasizing the term "brawling" as a method to keep women oppressed, needing the assistance of men to function properly.

However, the author states in 22:24 that an individual should not make friends with an angry man or follow a furious man. The writer also comments in 29:22 that an angry man stirs up strife and a furious man abounds in anger. The church must also address the negative behavior of men, as Scripture does not demarcate men from women in terms of destructive behavior; both are treated equal in this respect. Thus, leaders should not solely focus on brawling women to the exclusion of angry men. Although there are women who have earned the title of a brawler, the majority of IPV occurs against women at the hands of men. The author of Proverbs addresses negative behavior in both males and females. These passages of Scripture must not be utilized to instill fear in women to believe that they will end up lonely, isolated, and unsuitable for marriage. The church must present and implement a theology that reflects the positive nature of women and their significant contribution to the church, community, and society. The church must also be clear that women who express their opinions should not be viewed or perceived as contentious. Proverbs suggests that a wise husband listens to the advice and counsel of his wife, and should accept encouragement and correction from her when appropriate.

21. McKane, *Proverbs*, 554–54.

Proverbs 31:10–31

Proverbs 31:10–31 gives the depiction of a woman, referred to as Lady Wisdom, who provides wise counsel to men engaged in the process of selecting a suitable wife. The chapter begins with Lemuel's mother, who is a queen and ruler, giving advice to her son regarding women, and ends with the depiction of a virtuous woman who is to be desired by a husband.

The writer of 31:8–9 speaks up for the voiceless in the pathway of destruction and instructs individuals to judge righteously and plead the cause for the poor and needy. This is a powerful symbol of liberation theology; those who speak up for the oppressed and marginalized will also speak up for their wives and sisters, and females in general. There is a great need for the church to be cautious with this passage, making sure it is not being used to further subjugate women into a role of continued subservience to male leadership.

In 31:10–31 the writer concludes the book with an epilogue, an impressive acrostic poem giving honor and deference to a worthy woman who demonstrates and epitomizes the qualities and values identified with wisdom throughout the book. The passage is primarily addressed to an audience of young men on the threshold of maturity. The purpose of the chapter appears to be twofold in nature: first, *to offer counsel on the kind of wife a young man should seek*; second, *to advise young men to marry Lady Wisdom*, thus returning to the theme of chapters 1–9, comparing Lady Wisdom with a wife of noble character.[22]

The Black church in particular pays immense homage to this passage of Scripture as the hallmark and true representation of a godly woman who reveres the Lord and her husband. This passage is highly emphasized and quoted during women's meetings and Mother's Day services to depict the desired character of the pastor's wife, church mothers, and women of influence within the congregation.

However, Christians have misinterpreted the passage by placing emphasis on the behavior of women rather than the discernment of men to utilize wisdom in selecting a worthy marriage partner. The church has used this text to shame women into a place of submission and oppression for those who fail to live up to the qualities, traits, and characteristics of the woman of wisdom in the text. Women strive with all their strength to emulate this classy lady, only to experience disappointment if they do not

---

22. La Sor, Hubbard, and Bush, *Old Testament Survey*, 460.

please their husbands. The misinterpretation of the text sets women up to be vulnerable to abusive men rather than helping men find a woman who fears the Lord. The church must discontinue the utilization of this text to dominate women and allow the text to speak directly to the hearts of men, who, in turn, will understand that a woman never deserves to be abused, controlled, or subjugated. Men will comprehend that Lady Wisdom's price is far above rubies and a woman of this nature who fears the Lord should be praised by her husband.

Summary of Old Testament Texts

The Old Testament begins with the story of creation, culminating in the creation of Adam from the dust of the ground and the creation of woman from the rib of Adam and the dust of the earth. The OT is ripe with texts that have been used to support violence against women, and, at first glance, one would think this is the way of life intended for women. However, it is imperative to understand married life pre-and post-fall. Prior to the fall, Adam and Eve lived in unified harmony as a couple and with God, but after the fall a new structure entered into marriage and man was set to rule over woman and a woman's desire would be for her husband.

Fathers and husbands in the OT who exercised power to approve or disapprove the vow of a young daughter or wife opened the door for females to become codependent on males in OT Jewish culture and society. Likewise, Jewish women in OT times had no legal right to divorce their husbands, though they could be given a bill of divorce for any reason deemed appropriate by their husband.[23] The women were relegated to bearing children and being the primary nurturers and caretakers of the household, while holding a subordinate position in the family structure to males.

Males are expected to be protectors and providers of their families as well as bear responsibility for the spiritual direction and safety of the family unit. However, some men abused their role because of an unwillingness to love their wives as they loved themselves. The harmony that existed before the fall was transformed into a relationship of subservience and control, and the Black church, although far removed from Middle Eastern culture, in some respects continues in the traditions of the OT. It relies heavily on the hierarchical structure of marriage and inculcates this structure to congregants as the featured way of life for the family and women in the church.

23. Amram, *Jewish Law of Divorce*, 54–63.

This subordinate post-fall position paved the way for IPV and allowed the male power structure to cement itself as a permanent staple in church relationships. The Christian church must transition from a post-fall to pre-fall comprehension of marriage and utilize this concept to help eliminate abuse against women in the church.

The New Testament

The New Testament continues to address the issue of marriage, particularly in the Gospels and the writings of Paul and Peter. In the NT, the prophecy of the coming savior who will reconcile all things unto himself is fulfilled. Paul in particular speaks of being a new creation in Christ, transformed by the renewing of our minds so that we prove those things that are holy and acceptable to God. Paul constantly drives the point of being children of the kingdom, children of the day, and children of the light—a true reflection of the image of God in relationship to the world and the church. Although the Black church strongly believes in forming a strong relationship with God, domestic violence has left some darkness behind as the church continues to struggle with exposing the reality that abuse still exists in the church today. The church must embrace and adopt the NT understanding of marriage, particularly in the teachings of Jesus and Paul, to once again attain the same level of peace and tranquility enjoyed by Adam and Eve in the garden—a return to Eden, removing victimization, abuse, and control, and returning to harmonious relationships.

Matthew 19:1–9 and Mark 10:1–12

The passages of Matthew 19:1–9 and Mark 10:1–12 depict a scene in which a question is posed and an answer given regarding the subject of divorce and the law of Moses. The Pharisees, strict keepers and guardians of the law, posed a rhetorical question to Jesus about whether a man could put away or divorce his wife for any reason. The Pharisees were considered doctors of the law and fully aware of the question; however, their intent was to confuse and test Jesus on his understanding of the law.[24]

The Pharisees understood the nature of the question and the debate from opposing schools of thought; one argument from the school of

---

24. McCarren, *Matthew*, 102.

The Theological Foundations that Support IPV

Shammai contended that divorce was acceptable only for the wife's unfaithfulness, and the Hillel argument stated that a man could divorce his wife for as little as a spoiled dish.[25] The response that Jesus offered the Pharisees confirms the intent of the pre-fall narrative in Genesis regarding marital relationships.[26]

Previously, I proposed that Christians should acquire a pre-fall philosophy of marriage instead of a post-fall philosophy of marriage to assist men in understanding God's intent for marriage before the fall, and the goal of reducing IPV against women in the church. The answer Jesus gave in direct response to the rhetorical question sent shock waves through the Pharisees' understanding of the law concerning divorce and caused a firestorm of backlash. Jesus took them on a sojourn to the beginning, quoting Genesis 2 and making reference to Adam's revelation that the two are now one flesh and what God has joined together no human can unjoin.[27] The Pharisees asked another question of Jesus regarding men who write a bill of divorce under the law of Moses. Jesus gave another damaging response to their rhetorical question and stated that this commandment was written due to the hardness of the heart, but reminded the Pharisees that divorce was not the intent of God for marriage from the beginning.

Ron Clark comments that the Pharisees sought various reasons for divorce as a methodology to further victimize women and rabbis constructed a complex methodology of validating divorce that victimized women. Clark contends that Jesus' discussion of divorce did not address all forms of divorce but was a prohibition against the victimization of women. Jesus confronted the Pharisees regarding the oppression of women and encouraged men to seek reconciliation.[28] The Gospels, through the lens of Jesus, take the issue of marriage back in time to God's intent regarding marriage clothed in peace and harmonious living, without the hierarchical structure that came as a result of the fall.

The NT provides a different context for marriage, as Paul finds himself in a conundrum when confronted with issues of marriage and divorce in the Greco-Roman world, where women had more legal rights than Jewish women although they lived in the same geographic area. Paul addresses the issue of marriage from a slightly different perspective than the Gospels, and

25. Talbert, *Matthew*, 232–33.
26. Woodley, *Gospel of Matthew*, 191.
27. Evans, *Matthew*, 340–41.
28. Clark, *Freeing the Oppressed*, 87.

appears to endorse a post-fall understanding of marriage as well as approaching the issue from a Roman/Greek cultural purview. Although Paul discusses the man being the head of the women and calls for wives to submit to and obey their husbands, he calls for men to function in the image of Christ and places great emphasis on husbands modeling their responsibility and role in marriage after that of Christ in relation to the church. Thus, the majority of the responsibility in marriage is laid upon husbands, not wives; therefore husbands must function in a pre-fall image of marriage.

Scripture is clear that after the fall God asked where Adam was, not Eve, which is indicative that the husband is the leader who must give an account when issues arise. The responsibility of husbands and wives laid out by Paul was also patterned after the house codes in Hellenistic culture.

House Codes

The *haustefal*, or house codes, was a table of instructions for households in Hellenistic culture that guided management of the household for families living in Rome. House codes can be found in Scripture texts such as Colossians 3:18–19; 1 Corinthians 7 and 11; 1 Timothy 3:1–7; Titus; and 1 Peter 2:12. Scholars agree that Paul addressed the issue of the *haustefal* to demonstrate that the spread of Christianity posed no threat to house codes under Roman law. Paul encouraged believers that they should not walk in the same manner as the Gentiles, but use every opportunity to emanate the light of God in their marriages.[29]

The families of Hellenistic culture included husbands, wives, children, slaves, business partners, tenets, servants, and laborers all residing in the same house. The *haustefal* codes were hierarchal in nature according to Roman law, which stated that husbands were the head of the family. Although some women who were wealthy in society may have functioned as head of the household, the majority of households under Roman law were headed by males.[30] There is debate among scholars that the *haustefal* was internalized by the non-elite as a method to restrict and create separation from an economic paradigm. This debate has been nuanced by the fact that 90–95 percent of the population in Rome lived in crowded conditions of social stratification.

---

29. Arnold, *Ephesians*, 369–78.
30. Williamson, *Ephesians*, 220–21.

The Theological Foundations that Support IPV

However, whether rich or indigent, house codes applied to all, as this was a part of Roman culture and law.[31] Although the *haustefal* was a part of Roman law and culture, Paul encouraged Christians to walk in the light and demonstrate a godly pattern for marriage and family life. Paul states in Galatians 3:28 that there is neither male nor female in Christ, but also advocates that husbands are the head of the household. This does not connote that husbands are to behave as tyrannical dictators and treat their wives as slaves. Paul, through the direction of the Holy Spirit, addressed the issues from a historical context under the backdrop of the Hellenistic pagan practices in which women dominated and ruled over men, specifically in the temple of Diana, which we will discuss later in the chapter. The Black church must be encouraged to move beyond a post-fall image of marriage that subjugates women and leaves the door open for abuse and underreporting, and gravitate towards a pre-fall design of marriage to deconstruct the practice of male dominance that some Christians embrace. The church must delve into the Pauline texts and correctly exegete the passages, and move in the direction of harmonious relationship within a hierarchical family structure.

1 Corinthians 7:1–5 and 11:1–12

The city of Corinth was one of the most important cities in Greece during Paul's ministry. Corinth was known as a wealthy, proud, and wicked city located on a four-mile strip linked to the southern Peloponnese within the mainland of Greece, with two thriving seaports—Cenchraea on the east and Lechaeum on the west.[32]

The Corinthian church experienced issues such as factions, lawsuits, immorality, dubious practices, abuse of the Lord's Supper, and misuse of spiritual gifts.[33] The cities in which Paul ministered were vastly different from those of Jesus, who was sent to the lost sheep of Israel. The complications that Paul encountered in the church were entirely different than those of Jesus, and he had to trust the Holy Spirit to guide his interactions with congregants and assist newly converted Christians to embrace godly principles while living in a pagan society.[34] The issue of marital relationships

---

31. Tamez, *Early Christianity*, 30–33.
32. Toppe, *First Corinthians*, 1–3.
33. Bailey, *Paul Through Mediterranean Eyes*, 18.
34. Keener, *1–2 Corinthians*, 64–65.

was an area that Paul addressed with the Corinthian church with instructions on interaction, divorce, and singleness.

The passage in 1 Corinthians 7 is somewhat arduous to understand, as Paul distinguishes his voice from the Lord's voice. The chapter gives the appearance that Paul is responding to a letter that was written to him, probably from someone in the house of Chloe.[35] Paul begins by stating that every man and woman should have their own spouse to avoid fornication, and husbands and wives should render benevolence unto one another, as the wife does not have exclusive power over her body and the husband does not have exclusive power over his body. The verse implies that not only is there an obligation for the wife, but there is also an obligation for the husband, and it allows certain rights and ownership to wives. However, the verse implies that a husband had power over his wife's body, but a wife did not have power over her husband's body, thus, Paul implies a mutual sharing between husbands and wives.[36]

Paul states that husbands and wives are not to defraud or rob one another of intimacy, and to only abstain from intimacy by agreement. The implication in this verse seems to suggest that the husband cannot abstain from relations unless the wife consents and the husband cannot use his authority to defraud the wife. This understanding leads us to the term "debt," meaning each has a debt to pay to one another and each must satisfy that debt upon request, except for during fasting. However, the verse does not suggest that this can be done spitefully with malice; it conveys a message that both husband and wife must reach agreement for abstaining.[37]

Men, in most cases, are viewed as hyper-sexual initiators of sex, but the text also supports women to receive and enjoy sexual gratification in marriage.[38] Christendom tends to utilize this passage in a Jewish framework with the connotation that it is acceptable for the husband to refuse intimacy but it is unacceptable for the wife, thus placing women in a powerless position subordinate to men. Paul suggests that the balance of power must be shared with wives to foster harmonious marital relationships. This has echoes of a pre-fall relationship model proposed in Genesis, with woman at the side of man and not underneath man. The church should be encouraged to embrace the Pauline model in 1 Corinthians 7:1–5 to uplift

---

35. Johnson, *1 Corinthians*, 104–5.
36. Lockwood, *1 Corinthians*, 130–32.
37. Phillips, *Exploring 1 Corinthians*, 137–46.
38. Kovacs, *1 Corinthians*, 104–13.

The Theological Foundations that Support IPV

wives to a position of equality and teach men to understand the text from a Pauline perspective to confront issues of control and power against women in the church. This chapter heightens the status of women in marriage and elevates wives to a place of respectability beyond the post-fall perspective embraced by the Black church, specifically the Pentecostal church.

This can be a serious game changer for women to educate parishioners about the factors that lead to IPV and underreporting through the framework of incorrect exegesis that has contributed in some ways to the proliferation of abuse in the church.

The passage in 1 Corinthians 11:1–12 begins with a commandment from Paul to the Corinthians to be followers of him as he follows Christ. The Greek word for "follow," μιμητής, is understood to be an imitator, one who mimics Christ.[39]

Although Paul was not married, he set an example to the church of what it means to obey God in all aspects of life. The text then lists another commandment from Paul to keep the ordinances that he delivered to the Corinthian church. Paul describes the order of creation by stating that the head of every man is Christ, the head of the woman is the man, and the head of Christ is God. The transliteration in this text does not necessarily always imply a hierarchy in the marriage relationship.[40] However, the text gives insight into the origin of the woman, as she was created from the rib of a man.[41] Leon Morris suggests that Paul uses the phrase "head of the woman" not to depict authority over or rulership, but in the sense of origin or source.[42] Although the issue of head covering was due in part because of pagan practices, in verse 7 Paul states that the man should not cover his head as he is the image and glory of God and the woman is the glory of man, implying a similar meaning of "head" in verse 3 as origin or source.[43]

Paul continues in verse 8 with the theme of origin and source by stating that the man is not of the woman but the woman is of the man, and the man was not created for the woman but the woman was created for the man.[44] Paul makes an interesting observation in verse 11 by stating that the woman is nothing without the man and man nothing without the woman,

---

39. Kistemaker, *1 Corinthians*, 319.
40. Schenck, *1 & 2 Corinthians*, 151–55.
41. Pratt, *I & II Corinthians*, 177–82.
42. Morris, *1 Corinthians*, 149–51.
43. Nash, *1 Corinthians*, 328–29.
44. Garland, *1 Corinthians*, 522–23.

implying that men and women are demonstrating the restoration of God's creation in Genesis.[45] Rick Oster suggests that togas offered the impression that people sacrificed to pagan gods, as many art pieces depict males and females wearing hoods during sacrifices. Augustus and Julius Caesar were also depicted on coins and statues wearing a hood. The hood suggested that Caesar was not only lord, but a priest. When American television displays our president going to church, praying, or reading the Bible, the same message is portrayed. The toga had a hood that those in status used during acts of religious devotion.[46]

Bruce Winter comments that the hood seemed to be a sign of religious devotion that both men and women practiced. In the church it seems that there was an issue with what was right. To wear the hood suggested devotion, but to not wear it suggested disrespect and women who did not cover their heads were viewed as prostitutes.[47] For men, the issue was more divided, as Jewish males were opposed to covering their heads while Romans were expected to wear their hood in worship. Paul gives them a theological foundation: "They were in the image of God and should not hide their head." This provided an opportunity for the elite males to model humility in church.

Paul suggested that it was shameful for men to have long hair. For Paul, when men wore a hood (or had long hair) it was shameful conduct both culturally and theologically. Paul encouraged women to respect the culture and submit. However, Paul encouraged men to be somewhat countercultural. This text does not "put women in their place"; it actually challenges men to practice humility in their spiritual community.[48]

The Christian church should embrace a process that encourages mutual dependence in relationships between married couples. Paul made a strong suggestion that husbands and wives are encouraged to partner with one another and demonstrate that both originate from God, cooperating in agreement to the marriage covenant. Christendom must also recognize that everyone has an origin, a beginning or source of life, to which we give honor, praise, and glory. Children understand this best, as they honor and respect their parents, students honor and respect their instructors, and players honor and respect their coaches. Men in the church now

---

45. Wright, *1 Corinthians*, 138–41.
46. Oster, *1 Corinthians*, 230–40.
47. Winter, *After Paul Left Corinth*, 120.
48. Clark, *Better Way*, 106.

The Theological Foundations that Support IPV

have the responsibility to view women through the lens of creation and not as property they purchased and own. When the ownership component is removed from the equation and creation is placed at the core of marriage, men will understand that the greater responsibility is given to them as the head to lead in Christ as an example, not through domination, dictatorship, or authoritarianism. The task is to provide men with God-centered leadership that will encourage women to willingly follow and submit themselves under the headship of their husbands, which in turn will help marriages in the Black church progress towards a pre-fall state.

Colossians 3:18–19

The book of Colossians contains instructions for husbands and wives that are consistent with teachings to the Corinthian church regarding marriage roles and responsibilities. The first instruction for marriage, which Paul pronounces to women, is submission, ὑποτάσσεσθε; the term is understood to mean willingly subjecting yourself to your husband in the Lord.[49] The second instruction is for husbands to love their wives, ἀγαπᾶτε, which means to love, wish well, and show love for. Paul ends verse 19 by instructing husbands to refrain from bitterness against their wives.[50] The Greek word for bitterness, πικραίνεσθε, denotes harsh feelings or even resentment.[51] Although some scholars believe that this verse makes reference to a hierarchy, Paul does not redact the order he gave in Galatians 3:28, in which he states that there is neither male nor female, Jew nor Greek, slave nor free, but all are equal in God.[52] Paul admonishes wives to relinquish the temptation to behave in domineering ways toward their husbands and reminds husbands to ensure they love their wives as Christ loves the church.[53]

Peter, in 1 Peter 3:1–9, confirms the instructions of Paul for wives to be in subjection to their own husbands; however, in this text it is in regards to winning the unconverted pagan husband. Peter states in verse 7 that husbands are to dwell together with their wives according to knowledge; although the use of the word "knowledge" has been debated, most

---

49. Deterding, *Colossians*, 168–9.
50. Ibid.
51. Gupta, *Colossians*, 165–67.
52. Riches, *Galatians Through the Centuries*, 207–8.
53. Wright, *Colossians and Philemon*, 148–49.

theologians and scholars believe that the term denotes knowledge of the will of God for marriage.[54]

Peter then instructs husbands to give honor and praise to their wife as the more vulnerable vessel. "More vulnerable" is not necessarily used, as some theologians and scholars have concluded, in the sense of intellectual superiority of men over women, but in the sense that woman are weaker in physical stature as compared to men. The wife has a certain level of vulnerability as the weaker vessel but this does not carry the connotation that men should take advantage in certain situations; the inference is for husbands to be sensitive to their wife's vulnerabilities and provide protection, support, and comfort. The culminating result is that husbands will understand that wives are heirs together with them in the grace of life and that women were given spiritual authority in the garden of Eden, making the case for a pre-fall state of existence in marriage for husbands and wives.[55]

1 Timothy 3:1–4—Ruling the House Well

The Black church believes strongly in the notion of structure and order for men who believe they have been called to the ministry, particularly those who sense the call to lead a congregation. The pastor is expected to set the bar by having his own house in order as a prerequisite before providing leadership in the church. This places stress and burden on the pastor to keep things intact or suffer ridicule from congregants who would turn a deaf ear to his message because of a perception of him as a weak leader unable to control his household. This has somewhat contributed to IPV against women in the church as men utilize fear and domination tactics that lead to abuse and subjugation of women. The passage in 1 Timothy 3:1–4 uses the Greek term *episcope*, which means to administrator or one who oversees the affairs or business of a household.

Although the term has a direct translation of "bishop," we will use the definition of administrator and overseer without detracting from the origin of the word.[56] This is important to understand due to the many qualifications that administrators and overseers must demonstrate in order to lead the church. The overseer or administrator must not be a contentious leader with the predisposition to arguments and fights, and must be balanced,

54. Grudem, *1 Peter*, 142–43.
55. Chase and Holdren, *1–2 Peter, 1–3 John, and Jude*, 90–91.
56. Robinson and Wall, *Called to Lead*, 67–69.

sober, and tempered, demonstrating self-control.[57] The passage compares the household of the husband to the household of God; a husband who is incapable of managing his own house is not equipped to manage the house of God. Thus, the administrator has to clearly understand that if the attributes listed above are not exemplified in his home, he is unqualified to oversee God's house.[58]

The Greek term *prohistemi* not only suggests that men are to manage their homes well, but goes further and encourages men to be involved in the affairs and activities of their homes.[59] In the Black community, there is a saying that any man can be a daddy, but it takes a real man to be a father—one who is not only capable of producing babies, but who provides for them and is involved in every aspect of their lives as God is involved in every aspect of our lives. The notion of abuse, power, and control of women is not listed in the passage as a sign of godly administration.

Christendom must be cognizant of the relationship between the domestic and the ecclesiastic and seek ways to maintain a healthy balance by advocating that men first lead in the home to promote glory and honor to God as they prepare to lead in the church, as abuse against women in the home often leads to abuse against women in the church.

1 Timothy 2:9–15—To Usurp or Not Usurp Authority

The passage in 1 Timothy 2:9–15 has been utilized by the church to "keep women in check" while preserving the prestige of male dominance. The hallmark phrase in verse 11, "Let your women keep or learn in silence with all subjection," is the key text that pastors have utilized to quiet women, stripping away their voices and pushing them into the basement of humiliation, and not allowing women to function in leadership roles in the church. The church, for many years, has continually suggested that a woman should not teach or usurp authority over a man but remain in silence. The Christian church has a long history of misinterpreting the passage, as well as the other passages mentioned in this section, in a way that continues to victimize women.

Church leaders, due to a lack of education and theological training, in some respects, continue to mislead congregants through incorrect exegesis

---

57. Fiore, *Pastoral Epistles*, 72–83.
58. Collins, *I & II Timothy and Titus*, 83–85.
59. Clark, "Family Management or Involvement," 243.

to believe that women have no authority in the church. Followers of Christ must free women through correct exegesis of the text and tear down the walls of abuse and underreporting and restore women to their rightful place in the church. The historical context of the passage in 1 Timothy 2:9–15 is essential to understanding the message and direction that Paul gave to Timothy to convey to the church in Asia Minor. The apostle Paul instructed Timothy to inform women about appropriate conduct in the synagogue.

During this time, some women functioned inappropriately and exhibited unruly behavior towards men in the church. The Greek word *authentein* literally means: to act upon one's own perceived authority; to exercise authority; dictator and dominating.[60] The historical context related to this passage is critical to understanding the context of the passage. Most scholars believe that 1 Timothy was written by Paul during his extended time in Ephesus. The city of Ephesus was home to one of the most famous shrines, the temple of Artemis, the Greek name for Diana. This temple was a massive structure that dominated the entire area in Ephesus. The temple was headed by female priests, in comparison to a female-only cult where women ruled, dominated, and gained followers.[61] Thus, when Paul is instructing women to be silent in the church and not usurp authority over a man, he is referring to the behavior of some women in that particular synagogue who functioned as if they were in the temple of Diana.

They believed themselves to be the originator of man, as some Gnostics believed that woman was responsible for creation and the enlightenment of man.[62] N. T. Wright comments about the passage and states that the text is not suggesting that women cannot teach and learn in the church. He also makes strong reference to the passage encouraging the church, especially women, not to conduct themselves in the same manner as the women in the temple of Diana, who were bossy, domineering, and non-submissive.

Women must have their space to learn in the same manner as men, not forcing their way into leadership; both men and women must be free to develop gifts of learning and teaching given to them by God.[63] Although some believe that Paul was making a literal reference to women being under men,[64] this view is widely criticized by mainstream scholars simply

---

60. Guthrie, *Pastoral Epistles*, 88–89.
61. Towner, *Letters to Timothy and Titus*, 222–24.
62. Stott, *Message of 1 Timothy & Titus*, 75–77.
63. Wright, *1 Corinthians*, 25–27.
64. Hendriksen and Kistemaker, *Thessalonians, the Pastorals, and Hebrews*, 108–9.

on the basis that Paul's ministry featured many qualified women who accompanied him in ministry and even taught the word of God to men.[65] Some scholars state that the text should be applied in a universal setting, but modern scholarship believes that the text is not applicable to all contexts, as this is the only place in Scripture where women are asked not to teach or usurp authority over men. Therefore, the passage is addressing a specific issue and not the church universal, based in part on the fact that Paul's ministry displayed many women who taught alongside of him, and also in the ministry of Jesus.[66]

The issue was specific to women in the passage who were teaching heretical doctrine in the church and, when corrected, opposed the position of men, taking a bold and domineering stance even in their misinterpretation of Scripture.[67] The church has made significant progress in women's ministry, especially in the Pentecostal church. In the early COGIC history, it is a well-known fact that many churches were "worked out, preached out, and prayed out" by women. The meaning of this phrase makes reference to the many women who preached (although not from the podium), taught, and made intercession for the church while the pastor was en route from another church or to fill in the gap until a male pastor was appointed. Although more women are preaching from behind the sacred desk today, many women remain oppressed under the authority of men and are given a short leash to function in certain leadership roles.

Ephesians 5:21–32

The role of wives in the Black church receives significantly more attention than does the role of husbands. This is due in large part to cultural attitudes regarding the role of wives in the Bible that somehow still prevail thousands of years later in the West. The church has burdened women with extreme pressure to be perfect, to be the glue that holds everything together in the home, continuing to reinforce the notion of submission to their husbands. Christendom believes strongly in the Proverbs 31:10–31 passage, which elevates women to a place of honor, far above rubies, if she accomplishes the list of duties outlined in the passage. The woman who does not measure up to the standards of the chapter is accused of failing to be a good wife and

65. Black and McClung, *1 & 2 Timothy, Titus, and Philemon*, 57–60.
66. Krause, *1 Timothy*, 50–70.
67. Ibid.

a woman pleasing to her husband. Ephesians 5:21–32 suggests a different message in terms of the role of the husband, which moves the substantial weight of responsibility for marriage from the wife to the husband. Harold W. Hoehner states that in this passage there are 41 words used for women but 116 words used for men in the depiction of the roles of each spouse.[68] This clearly implies that although the success of the marriage is contingent upon both husband and wife fulfilling their designated roles, the husband has the preponderance of responsibility in the marriage.

Francis Foulkes states that although male and female are equal in the eyes of God, in the house codes of marriage and family there must be a head. The marriage between a husband and wife mirrors that of God's relationship to the church as reflected in the language of the prophets.[69] The roles and responsibilities of marriage related to its success are vested in the head; the male is strongly encouraged to function in the marriage in the same manner as Christ with the church. The act of submission is a voluntary act by the wife, who conducts herself accordingly simply because the husband fulfills his duty as the head of the house. The text strongly advocates for mutual submission between husbands and wives. Paul does not divert from the house codes present during his time of ministry, but he also does not use the structure of the house codes to permit male dominance and the subjugation of women.

Although some scholars believe that Ephesians 5:21 makes reference only to previous verses, more recent scholarship suggests this verse is applicable to the passages that describe the roles of husbands and wives, thus pointing forward as well as backward in the text.[70] The pattern of submission flows in this manner: C (wife) is submissive to B (husband) as B is submissive to A (Christ), thus C and B are both submissive to A and to one another.

The wife yields to her husband as her husband yields to Christ, thus breaking down attempts at domination and control, but allowing submission in freedom as all parties yield to their respective heads.[71] The wife submits herself to her husband in obedience to God and not simply because of the commandment of the husband. The Christian values and attitudes of

---

68. Hoehner, *Ephesians*, 132–35.
69. Foulkes, *Ephesians*, 161–70.
70. Fowl, *Ephesians*, 186–87.
71. Barth, *Ephesians 4–6*, 608–14.

women are the catalyst for submitting to their husbands.[72] The commands for husbands also involve two feminine words, "nurture" and "cherish," which are indicative of the instruction of husbands to be supportive of their wives as well as to admire and reverence them. The church has used this text to demand full control of wives, especially using Ephesians 5:23, where it states "in everything." This has taken on a very different meaning than the intent of the text, as men bypass their obligation of submission unto the Lord while demanding that their wives fall into full submission to their authority. Christendom must abandon the principles of dictatorship that support abuse and oppression of women and adopt a panoramic submission in which husband and wife submit to one another as both submit to the Lord through godly obedience. James Boice states that the standard for husbands is higher than for wives and lists five verbs in Ephesians 5:25–28 that add support to his argument: to love, to give oneself, to make holy and set apart, to cleanse, and to present one's wife. These five verbs set the stage for how women submit to their husbands through the fulfillment of these five verbs by the husband.[73]

The Greek word for love in these verses, *agape*, suggests a meaning of unselfish and unconditional love, admonishing the husband to love his wife for who she is and the gifts and graces she brings into the marriage, expressing an earnest desire for and appreciation of his wife. This term for love involves a husband who loves his wife so much that he is willing to sacrifice himself, following the pattern of Christ and the church.

This is the love that a husband should demonstrate for his wife just as Christ demonstrated his love for humanity on Calvary.[74] The love of a husband for his wife should be broad and run deep as the ocean waters so that, if necessary, the husband sacrifices his own prestige, body, and needs in order to fully care for his wife. The husband must give himself willingly; as the writer of Hebrews mentions, Jesus willingly requested that a body be prepared for him to enter the earth to redeem humanity.[75] Jesus stated that "no man takes his life, but he lays it down," implying his willingness to sacrifice himself as a true shepherd for the sheep (John 10:18).[76]

---

72. Muddiman, *Epistle to the Ephesians*, 258–59.
73. Boice, *Ephesians*, 199–202.
74. Slater, *Ephesians*, 156–57.
75. Long, *Hebrews*, 160.
76. Brant, *John*, 162.

The husband must also be willing to give of himself in order for the wife to be sanctified and cleansed. Sanctification and cleansing are a result of the sacrifice and death of Christ; the church is set apart and cleansed by the blood of Christ.[77] Husbands must sanctify and cleanse their wives by their sacrifice, setting them apart as the beloved of God. The imagery of cleansing is significant as it connotes the idea of bathing and washing the bride. Although some scholars believe that cleansing refers to baptism, most scholars agree that the term "cleansing" makes reference to literally bathing in water.[78]

The last verb that depicts the role of the husband in marriage is that of one who presents his wife to himself as a glorious and radiant wife just as the church is presented in glory and radiance to Christ. This speaks of the artistic beauty of the bride as a young, attractive woman, morally pure with no spots, wrinkles, or blemishes. When husbands fulfill their roles, duties, and obligations by the five five verbs listed above and on the previous page, this is how their wives will look.[79] Wives can feel beautiful if their husbands follow one principle, outlined in Ephesians, which simply states that husbands must love their wives as their own bodies. Paul states that no man (husband) hates his own flesh; therefore, husbands are prohibited from hating their wives. The text refers back to Genesis 2:24 and further implies that, upon consummation of the marriage, husband and wife become one and what the husband inflicts upon the wife he inflicts upon himself. Therefore, it is immensely imperative that husbands understand this mystical union as the culmination for the test of true love for their wives, loving their wives as they love their neighbors.[80]

Summary of New Testament Texts

New Testament passages regarding marriage must be understood in light of their historical context and meaning. The church in some respects has failed to include the background of the NT passages to provide a balanced and educated understanding to congregants regarding the issue of husbands and wives. Ephesians 5 lists 116 words in its requirements for men compared to 41 words for women, indicating that the responsibility for the success of a marriage falls on the shoulders of husbands.

77. Best, *Ephesians*, 253–54.
78. Thielman, *Ephesians*, 382–83.
79. Liefield, *Ephesians*, 146–47.
80. O'Brien, *Letter to the Ephesians*, 426–27.

The issue of the husband as the head has been a major bone of contention in the church due to the lack of education about the texts discussed throughout the chapter. Although Paul utilized the house codes related to marriage as he provided direction to the Roman-Greco citizens who became Christians, it is clear that Paul disapproved of husbands who attempted to dominate and control their wives. Husbands were clearly instructed to love their wives as Christ loves the church and gave himself for the salvation of the church.

Conclusion

The Black church must embrace a restoration of the pre-fall notion of marriage in Genesis 2, in which equality existed between males and females, and utilize this as a prototype to eliminate abuse, control, oppression, and IPV against women in the church. Although the notion and variation of house codes exists in the Black community and church, this must be understood in light of the history and culture of the time Paul wrote to the Christians in Asia Minor. The house codes were never intended to replace the notion of godly principles of marriage. The relationship between husband and wife should always model the relationship between Christ and the church, founded on the basis of unconditional love. The Black church has utilized these texts to abuse, control, and subjugate women rather than correctly exegete the text to promote healthy relationships and marriages. The marriage relationship must mirror the relationship between God and the church; in doing this we can assist in reducing IPV and assist women with reporting abuse. Pastors and leaders must understand that it is in the best interest of their congregations and church ministries to place more emphasis on addressing domestic violence among parishioners. This carries an immense theological mandate in terms of a shift in how the ministries shepherd families impacted by abuse.

Further, pastors and church leaders must be encouraged to understand the theological impact of not addressing IPV. The theological aspect of abuse is imperative for church members in terms of discipleship, healing, restoration, growth, and ongoing development. God cares about IPV, therefore the church should care about IPV and the ramifications for families who experience abuse. The church must embrace the same level of care as God and understand that it is in the collective best interest to help congregants who experience domestic violence.

Chapter 4

Focus Group Interviews

THE HISTORICAL ASPECTS OF IPV steeped in the Black church tradition continues to have a negative impact on women and reinforce abuse. The notion of domestic violence in the church is immersed in the traditions and cultures of how biblical texts are understood and applied to different facets of life. Historically, the notion of marriage has not been viewed through the lens of the marginalized, thus leaving the door open for continued victimization of women in the church.

This section will consist of qualitative research from a focus group in which eight different women were presented with six questions regarding their own experiences with IPV, developed by Ron Clark and myself. The real names of each woman will be concealed to protect their identities at their explicit request. The questions are as follows:

1. What can you tell me about your experience that will help me understand what you went through?
2. Did you report the abuse to anyone? Why or why not?
3. What was the impact on you, your family, and the congregation?
4. Who were some of the people who helped you along the way? What did they do?
5. What were some of the actions of people that were not helpful to you?
6. What advice would you give to women today who encounter IPV?

Focus Group Interviews

Focus Group

The focus group consisted of eight women ranging in age from twenty-nine to sixty-two. Six of the eight women remarried after experiencing IPV and two of the women have chosen to remain single after experiencing abuse in marriage.

The ethnicity of the women is African American and they all attend predominantly Black churches with pastors of the same ethnicity. Three of the women were married to pastors, two of the women were married to associate ministers, one was married to a deacon, and two were married to non-leadership males in the church. All of the women have at least one child and have graduated from high school; four of the women graduated from college and two of the women obtained a master's degree.

Focus Group Interview Questions

1. What can you tell me about your experience that will help me understand what you went through?

The majority of the responses from the women confirmed that their experiences were immensely devastating and resulted in tremendous amounts of stress, anxiety, physical, and emotional pain. Most of the survivors reported that the devastation was arduous to endure on a daily basis while maintaining employment, their households, and their children intact. This tripod approach proved to be a tough balancing act while portraying the perfect family to the church and public. The thought of living a "double life" proved to be a great strain for most of the survivors, fulfilling that role during church services, women's meetings, and other church events that mandated their presence. The survivors stated that it was very difficult to sit through a Sunday morning service while their husbands functioned in ministry, delivered sermons, prayed for parishioners, served Communion, and adorned the holy garments and vestures of the church. There was one survivor in particular that shared her story of how her husband taught a sermon series on "The Successful Christian Marriage" while abuse was present in their home.

She said, "It was the most difficult sermon series to listen to, as my husband portrayed his own marriage as the example for other married couples in the church." She stated that the conversation during the drive home was filled with excitement from her husband, who had received good reviews from congregants about the sermon series, while those same people had no idea of the issues transpiring in the home of their pastor.

The survivors stated that there was a high level of mental anguish encountered daily as a result of trying to discover a methodology to avoid IPV. Most of the survivors stated that they spent countless hours devising strategies to avoid being abused by their husbands. The strategies ranged from having his favorite meal cooked when he arrived home or massaging his shoulders if they sensed he was stressed or angry due to external factors at work or in the church to avoid being the indirect object of his anger and frustration. Some of the women stated that they would begin finding tasks to do around the house to give the appearance of being busy, making their husbands feel like kings in hope that they were just too tired after a hard day of work to abuse them.

Three survivors even said that they would tell their husbands that they were experiencing symptoms of pregnancy to prevent abuse from occurring for a period of time. When asked about the husband's suspicions of the pregnancy, they would simply state that they lost the baby due to stress. Another survivor stated that she would pretend to be sleeping when her husband arrived home, hoping that he would not wake her and start with the verbal abuse. Nearly all of the women confirmed that fear was one of the most dreadful weapons used to control and abuse.

The Weapon of Fear

The survivors confirmed that fear was the main weapon utilized to control them, includiung fear of reporting abuse to anyone, especially law enforcement. The women stated that fear was so ingrained into their thought patterns that it dominated their mode of thinking and their ability to make decisions or take actions despite knowing the appropriate manner to address the issue. The notion of fear stripped their ability to think broadly and forced them to focus on protecting their children from the daily horror they experienced. One survivor in particular recited the mental suffering as a result of the constant fear of her husband's volatile behavior, and she described how she would shake when she heard his key unlock the door and watch her husband enter the home, not knowing what type of mood he was in or when the abuse would begin. She stated that the abusive behavior would begin after strenuous board meetings in which he was denied a request by the board to start a program or increase funding. Another survivor stated that fear pushed her to the brink of depression and suicide as she felt helpless and unable to overcome the terror of her husband's thunderous voice and violent outbursts. She stated that the only thing that kept her from suicide was her children.

One woman also reported that her husband was an outstanding member of the community serving on several high-profile boards and was a respected voice among his peers, community, and civic leaders. She stated that she felt she had no one to turn to who would listen to her story because of his standing in the community among the power brokers and elites; a few of these elite power brokers attended services at their church. The fear she described entailed losing her children if she attempted to report because of her husband's political and social connections within the community.

The constant fear of losing her children if she reported held her in checkmate and made her unable to counter her fear. She stated that her husband would threaten her with losing the children periodically if she ever disclosed and this held her tongue captive for many years. Yet another survivor stated that fear had literally paralyzed her and forced her to accept the abuse although she believed in her heart that IPV was wrong. She stated that her battle was not with her abusive husband but with her internal fear to escape abuse. Although she remained in the relationship for a few years beyond the recognition of her inner battle with fear, she finally had the courage to report to someone in the church, flee the situation, and obtain a better life with her children. The women reaffirmed that fear was one of the most important weapons in the repertoire of abusers. They further confirmed that the weapon of control was equal to the weapon of fear.

The Weapon of Control

The women overwhelmingly confirmed that control was the twin sibling of fear, depicting the notion of control as comparable to incarceration behind cell bars. The survivors stated that almost every aspect of their lives was controlled by their husbands. They stated that they were told when to cook, when to serve, in some cases when to eat, when to leave, when to return, and which individuals to communicate with. The control, in some cases, extended to complete domination of life both inside and outside the home as well as all decisions for the family, finances, and relationships. The women confirmed that because of fear they handed over complete governance to their husbands and most times did not question him even if they were aware that certain requests were dubious.

One survivor said she was consistently asked by her husband to write checks even though she was aware there was not enough money in the account to cover the checks. Another survivor stated that her husband dominated every aspect of the finances to the extent that she never knew how much money was in the account. She was given a certain amount of money to spend per week to cover shopping for groceries, clothes for the children, and other household items.

The women stated that in some instances control was gained very subtlety and deceptively over time by establishing and building trust. One survivor reported that her husband was so astute in handling the household finances that she never imagined he would change his behavior and become such a dominating force in that area. She stated that she was literally stripped of knowing anything about the finances and her spending was micromanaged down to the very penny. Further, if there was anything outside of the normal order of spending, she was questioned and scolded by her husband. She stated that she lived in constant fear of overspending or not having a good explanation of money spent above the allotted amount.

Another survivor stated that her husband controlled the finances of the church and the home, which meant that she was not allowed to know too much about money and was told to appreciate the nice living that she had been provided. Her husband travelled extensively as an evangelist and received significant amounts in honorariums, but she never knew his yearly income. One survivor shared how she lived a lavish lifestyle and had everything at her disposal—clothes, shoes, hats, purses, cars, etc. However, they were given to her as gifts to encourage her not to report abuse and to regain her trust. There were a few women who also shared the same experience of receiving what they referred to as gifts for silence. Most survivors stated that it was difficult to flee the abusive situation without access to finances, inclusive of credit or debit cards.

When asked about the possibility of residing in a shelter, the survivors with male children stated that it is virtually impossible to find a shelter that will accept male children over a certain age. The women stated that most individuals who have never experienced IPV fail to understand that money plays a vital role in fleeing abuse and having the ability to care for children.

Overall, the survivors identified the major themes of fear and control as defining their experience and stated that they were the two most powerful weapons that their husband's utilized to maintain dominance over nearly all important areas of their lives and the family.

2. Did you report the abuse to anyone? Why or why not?

Fear

The majority of survivors stated that they did not initially report the abuse to anyone, especially family or church members. The women said they often considered reporting abuse, but fear was the main reason they hesitated. The fear they described centered on retaliation for reporting or attempting to report, especially to family or law enforcement. Most survivors stated that if they could have filed a report without being caught or suspected by their husbands they would have attempted to leave in the beginning of the abuse. One survivor said she was so overwhelmed with fear that she erased the very thought of reporting against her husband and kept the focus on her children. Most survivors reported that a major factor of not reporting was the potential impact to the church and ministry, along with the ramifications of life after reporting. For some, their husband's ministries had become quite successful through much effort, trials, and suffering, and years of painstaking sacrifice to see the ministry reach its pinnacle.

Although most survivors were employed in the secular arena, they stated that ministry and church work was the priority that defined their lives. The battle between reporting and potentially losing the ministry that was everything to their husband's livelihood was the catalyst of silence for not reporting.

One survivor stated that she was afraid to report because of her husband's strong standing in the community and his respect among ministry colleagues. She stated that she refused to take the chance of losing her children, with the possibility that full custody would be granted to her husband as she was unemployed at the time. The discussion with the survivors transitioned back to the subject of the fear of retaliation, with most survivors commenting that the pain, mental agony, and suffering served as a reminder of what could happen if they spoke about abuse outside of the home. One survivor reported that her husband choked her and slammed her against their bedroom wall and threatened that it would be worse if she ever hinted about the abuse to anyone. She stated that the incident occurred after her husband drilled her with questions about a discussion at a women's church meeting. She stated that it was customary for him to question her about topics discussed in meetings to ensure that no information was shared outside the home. The incident left her petrified and although she entertained the thought of reporting, she was very nervous to make any attempt to report IPV.

One survivor stated that she did report abuse to law enforcement and the legal community but received very little assistance to help her address the issue. The first time she involved law enforcement, they determined that it was a simple domestic dispute and advised her to separate from her husband for one night and have a cooling down period. She stated that her understanding was that law enforcement's decision was determined due to there being no physical violence and no visible marks on her body. Law enforcement determined that it was a minor disagreement between them that did not escalate enough to require outside involvement. She stated that the officers did not offer much assistance or ask questions to get to the root of the problem. They remained on site until her husband got some clothes and then departed.

The theme that continues to weave through the first two questions involves fear: fear of the overall experience, fear of reporting, and retaliation from the abuser. The survivors said fear is such a powerful weapon in the hands of abusers and the public has difficulty understanding how fear cements women in the ground and shackles their hands and feet from taking the appropriate action. They stated that in the midst of experiencing abuse, the main focus was survival and eliminating the possibility of losing their children.

Shame

The survivors overwhelmingly stated that shame is an immensely powerful force that also prevents women from reporting IPV. They stated that living multiple lives was immensely strenuous; one life at home, another life at church, and another life in the public eye. One survivor stated that she wanted to report to the church and district superintendent, but was forced to think about the shame she would potentially encounter after many years of reporting to the church that all is well in the home and that the Lord keeps on doing great things as one-liners to avoid the real issues. The survivors posed questions as part of the discussion with one another. "How was

I to face my family with these issues? How could I tell anyone in the church about my problems when my husband is the senior pastor?"

One survivor said there were very few occasions that she could be around other pastors' wives and listen to them discuss the success of their marriages while her marriage was laden with abuse. The external shame was only matched by the shame experienced at home. The survivors stated that their experience of shame was long and deep in their minds and hearts.

Most of the survivors stated that the internal shame suffered at the hands of their husbands was demoralizing. They stated that a significant majority of the shame experienced came through verbal abuse that directly attacked their character, intelligence, and competence. They were made to feel inferior while being treated like immature children. The verbal onslaughts continued daily as their husbands were relentless with statements, words, and phrases that belittled, degraded, and humiliated them.

One survivor told a story of how most every decision she made was questioned by her husband and he asked her to provide a reasonable explanation as to why she was late coming home or arriving at her destination. She stated that she was expected to call her husband when she arrived at work or her family's home. The goal was to monitor her every move and break down her ability to think, thus making her solely dependent on her husband. She stated that shame, condemnation, and guilt gripped her mind and she felt extremely dehumanized as she heeded to every call of her husband. At times, she stated that she experienced deep depression dealing with the shame, losing her self-confidence, and believing the derogatory statements her husband hurled at her for years.

Another survivor stated that her husband utilized a strategy of posing questions to make her feel stupid and ignorant; they were questions that she could not answer due to the fact that he was highly educated and she only possessed a high school diploma. She stated that it was agonizing to engage in discussions with him as something in the conversation would trigger his anger. She further stated her husband methodically and systematically deprogrammed her ability to think, which triggered shame and condemnation and shut down the conversation.

The survivors stated that when shame is experienced it pushes them into a state of immense low self-esteem to the extent that they severely lack the ability to feel good about themselves and constantly question their every move to avoid abuse. They depicted a process in which the shame and lack of self-confidence is difficult to cope with once they start to believe the deprecating statements made about them, especially those spoken in front of their children, family, or friends. One survivor stated that the words spoken struck so deep in her mind that all she heard were the words "stupid," "dumb," "incompetent," and "ignorant." Each time she would make a mistake, she would jokingly make comments such as "Oh, I'm sorry, I'm just dumb today" or "How could I be so incompetent and stupid? That was so easy." She stated that she made these comments at work and church; although this was outside of her normal behavior, no one at work or church noticed the negative statements she made regarding herself, or they brushed them off as silly comments made in fun.

The major factor that the survivors confirmed regarding shame and not reporting was the process of how shame lead to bouts with depression, misery, despair, and hopelessness.

The amount of dejection took its toll on many of the survivors, who stated that they no longer lived; instead, they just decided to exist, make no waves, and survive for the sake of their children. They said that life was drained out of them, leaving them with no reason to lift themselves up from the ashes to live again and enjoy life. Life could not be enjoyed because of the constant shame and blame for nearly everything that went wrong, even if they had no part in the matter. The survivors stated that blame was another strong weapon to keep the focus off the real issues of the abuser and place the emphasis indirectly on them. The survivors stated that shame is still difficult to overcome today, but they continue to work through the pain.

3. What was the impact on you, your family, and the congregation?

Impact on the Survivor

The survivors overwhelmingly stated that the impact of abuse was enormous from a mental, physical, and emotional standpoint. They stated that the mental distress was very severe in the midst of holding the family together and keeping the issue hidden from the children. The mental and emotional aspects drained their energy, took away their will to live, and stripped them of the little hope they clung to that the abuse would end one day soon. The survivors stated that the impact of domestic violence resulted in mild to severe depression and impaired their ability to complete simple tasks at work, home, and church. They reported often forgetting tasks they started and could not remember what things they had to complete. They also indicated that each day it became more difficult to find the strength and the will to live, make it through another day, and care for the children.

The survivors reported both thoughts of suicide and suicide attempts, as well as a loss of interest in most activities with friends, as their lives centered on the church and home. The survivors stated that it was difficult to form relationships out of fear that the issues in the home would be revealed, resulting in more abuse.

One survivor talked about her issues with depression as a result of the abuse. She stated that her husband treated her very cruelly and constantly berated her at home although he said nice things about her in front of the congregation. She stated that she spent many days battling the sadness she experienced from the harsh words and yelling that caused her to be moody with her children. The survivor stated that this impacted her emotionally and psychologically as she witnessed her children attempt to understand her emotional imbalance and mental instability. The children walked on eggshells and could feel the tension in the home. They became slightly aware of the issues, but they kept quiet to prevent more problems.

Impact on the Family

The survivors stated that the impact on the family was not overt; the children, especially young children, were not always aware of the issues, although they could sense that things were edgy between their parents. The survivors stated that it was difficult to conceal the issues from the children as they grew older and understood that their mother was obscuring the abuse to protect their father. The children respected their father and appreciated him for taking care of their needs, but embraced their mother to help her as best as they could to manage the problems. One survivor talked about the day her daughter observed her husband scolding her for not picking him up from the airport on time as she explained that she was held up in traffic due to a bridge closure.

She stated that her daughter eventually told her siblings about the incident, which was eventually revealed to her parents as well as family on both sides of the aisle. She described several meetings and interventions that occurred with her husband and both sides of the family that ended with no resolution. Family on both sides attended the church that her husband pastored and chose to arrange private interventions to avoid the information being leaked to the congregation or community.

One woman discussed her longing to have relationships with friends inside and outside of the church, but she was fearful to develop those associations so she could protect her husband and the church. There was a constant battle to establish boundaries although she desired to form a bond with the pastor's wife and other woman in the church. In her mind there was a constant struggle on whether to engage and build rapport with other women or remain the faithful and dedicated wife and mother supporting the household and her husband as he tended to the responsibility of the church.

There were a few survivors who discussed having good relationships with women in the church and community, and most had strict boundaries in conversations about family and home life. One survivor talked about how she utilized Scripture to discourage a discussion about IPV. She stated that she often quoted Psalms 105:10, "Touch not my anointed and do my prophets no harm," to prevent women from mentioning anything about domestic violence and the pastor. She was always able to divert the conversation away from her to focus on abuse issues with other women in the church. She stated that it was very hard to trust due to hearing stories of how women trusted others with confidential information only to discover that their secret was exposed, causing their abuse to become worse.

The survivors also stated that their children had an immensely difficult times understanding why they could not have sleepovers or spend too much time with friends. One survivor said it was very hard to explain to her small children about living such a private and secluded life in order to elude revealing the issues in the home.

Another survivor stated that her husband was a mastermind at using events such as birthday parties, fun activities, and pool parties to present the picture-perfect family in front of their children's friends, who were members of the church along with their parents. She stated that her husband would BBQ for his children's friends and make banana splits and rootbeer floats so the friends would return home and tell their parents about the good time they had at the pastor's home. She stated that the façade irritated her, but there was nothing she could do to stop the perception that he built for himself, at the expense of the children, to the congregation and community. The survivors also discussed the impact on the family years after the abuse occurred, stating that their children revealed what they knew and the effects in terms of dating, relationships, marriage, and the perception of God and spirituality.

Focus Group Interviews

Impact on the Congregation

One survivor told a story of how the congregation was made aware of the IPV issues in her home in front of the family. She told the story of an incident that occurred in the home one Saturday evening in which law enforcement had to intervene. Her husband was taken into custody, posted bail, and was released the next morning. She and the children went to church the next morning and she was not surprised that her husband showed up and took his seat on the platform to review the Sunday school lesson.

However, during children's church, one of the children asked her son about his day on Saturday and he responded by saying the police came to my house and took my daddy away. The survivor stated that the information rocked the church heavily and they desired to know how long the issues had been occurring and what steps were being put in place to address the issue. The congregants finally understood that the pastor's wife didn't wear sunglasses in the sanctuary due to the bright lights causing migraines, like her family had always said. The survivors stated that the impact on the church varied from church to church, especially in terms of how the issue is addressed among the elder's board, deacon boards, and church administration. They stated the variation is contingent upon the denomination and culture of the organization, and more importantly the leadership's ability to properly address the issue once it rises to their level.

One survivor stated that her church was devastated when the issue of abuse came to light and many congregants decided to leave and attend other churches. The church was divided between the pastor, pastor's wife, and the children; this caused great disruption in church services. She stated that the associate pastors preached on Sunday mornings, taught Bible study, and led the worship services while she, her husband, and the children attended individual and family counseling. The survivor stated that the division in the church was easily recognizable, as most congregants held to their convictions. The reputation of the church suffered greatly in the community as most individuals were aware of the issues once the information was discussed in public.

One survivor stated that in her church congregants acted as though the issue had no effect on them and many reported that they did not know what to do or how to respond when the abuse was revealed to the congregation. She stated that most parishioners continued with their ministry tasks and assignments, leaving church administration, leadership, and the pastor's family to deal with the problem. She also stated that congregants were nervous to express any concern for fear that they would be punished by God for saying anything that could be perceived as negative against the pastor. This was true even though they were confident that IPV occurred. She stated that this was disappointing because she finally grasped the span of her husband's control that started in the home and extended to the church.

The survivors stated that many members in church ministries desire to confront the issue head on and believe that pastors should meet with the entire congregation to explain the details of what happens in IPV cases. Most survivors stated that most pastors will refuse to meet with the church and discuss the issue, choosing instead to meet with a select group of ministers and leaders who support them. The impact on the church was immensely frustrating as church members felt that they received more information from external sources than church leadership, which left many in a state of uncertainty regarding the process of how domestic abuse was being addressed. They stated that although some of their husbands stepped down from preaching and ministry assignments for a period of time, they continued to function as the head of the church or department and direct day-to-day operations. This was disturbing for some women to observe their husbands continue in ministry in lieu of attending and participating in individual and family counseling sessions.

The survivors stated that many congregants looked to leadership above the pastor's level to address the issues, such as a district official or bishop, but stated that they received little assistance. Many times parishioners were left with little to no information about the outcome, resolution, or details of the circumstances. The perception of the church was that things were concealed to protect the pastor from shame, embarrassment, and exposure.

There was virtually no transparency throughout the process except a request for prayers and a stern message from leadership forbidding individuals to discuss the issue outside the church. The survivors stated that congregants had become dispirited as they were not allowed to have any contact with the pastor, his wife, or their children as long as the issue was ongoing. The survivors reiterated that most congregations suffered tremendously due to a lack of communication throughout the entire process, only to see the pastor return to the pulpit and preach without giving any details of the outcome. They stated that communication is the key for addressing any issue, especially IPV, early in the process. While the survivors acknowledged that the impact on the congregation was significant, the family suffered in unimaginable ways, especially women who were bombarded with questions and phone calls about the abuse and their plan to address it.

4. Who were some of the people who helped you along the way? What did they do?

The Trust Factor

The survivors stated that there were a few individuals who wanted to help and provide support during their time of abuse. The issue of individuals providing assistance was, in some cases, buried under the inability to openly discuss the matter due to the position of their husbands in the church and fear. This made it extremely difficult to seek help without exposing their husbands and subjecting their children to undue hardships as a result of the circumstance. The survivors stated that it was very difficult to trust individuals in the church or community with sensitive information because of fear that individuals would report to law enforcement before the victims were ready or able. The issue of trust was huge among survivors as many sensed they had nowhere to turn for help. They constantly weighed the options of asking for support but could not decide the best course of action; however, there were a few survivors that did have individuals along the way to help as they endured the abuse.

Emotional Support

One survivor stated that she had a close confidant she trusted to disclose the abuse and receive support. She stated that her friend approached her after she noticed a small bruise on her lower arm as they were in the women's restroom at church. Her friend provided much-needed emotional support through listening, with no response, suggestions, or directives about how to deal with the problem. The survivor stated that her confidant respected the boundary, although there were times she knew her friend desired to intervene and help her escape. She also said that her confidant's patience proved to be very helpful in allowing her time to think about the issue and determine the best course of action while protecting her children.

Having the space to envision an escape plan without feeling overwhelmed with suggestions from her confidant decreased the confusion and anxiety that plagued her mind daily. She further stated that her confidant, who never experienced IPV, attended some trainings and seminars to better understand abuse and the impact on families. This willingness by her confidant to understand the plight of abused women spoke volumes about her commitment and dedication to her and the children.

The survivors also discussed turning to family and congregants to divulge their situation and problems, and described some good processes and negative processes for how things were handled in both contexts.

Active Listening

One survivor shared a story with the group of how the associate pastor's wife was her close friend and keenly aware of the IPV in her marriage. She stated that her friend witnessed the abuse on several occasions and was stunned to discover that her pastor, who was great friends with her husband, acted in such a disrespectful manner in her presence. She stated that her friend made her husband aware of the issues, but voiced concern about addressing the issue with the pastor or reporting it to church leaders in fear that he would expose the pastor and be punished for reporting abuse. The survivor stated that her friend desired desperately to report, but out of respect for her she remained silent, walking hand in hand with the victim throughout the abuse. She stated that her friend cried with her many nights and was torn when the pastor took to the podium to tell the congregation how much he loved his wife and children, when she knew his wife suffered tremendously behind closed doors. She stated that her friend was a master at listening and avoided the mistake of blaming her for not taking more action."

The survivors stated that having a confidant to actively listen to their problems is enormous in terms of allowing time to release some of the pain as they continued to experience the horrific effects of domestic abuse.

They stated that far too many times individuals who desire to help are more concerned about the abuse than the victim and desire to play the role of hero instead of understanding the present circumstance. The survivors stated that the art of active listening is one of the most invaluable tools that confidants can employ when assisting victims. The survivors confirmed that too much talking distracts from understanding the mindset of victims and their needs as they progress toward an exit plan. They agreed that education is supreme in assisting victims of domestic violence.

Education

The survivors agreed that blaming victims for failure to take action to protect themselves and their children could be damaging to victims attempting to flee abuse. They reiterated the importance of education, which was shared previously in the discussion by a survivor who expressed appreciation of her confidant educating herself about IPV. They stated that one way to assist is for confidants and friends to develop a list of available resources to assist them when they finally gain enough courage to confront family violence and escape. They stated that most individuals who desired to help had great intentions, but due to a lack of education they caused more harm than good by taking charge of the situation and making decisions for victims, functioning in a similar capacity as the abuser, with controlling and directive behavior. The survivors reiterated the importance of congregants, family, and friends obtaining education and not imposing their will on victims. The survivors shared how their loved ones acted out of sincere concern but failed to understand that swift action is not always the best response when dealing with family violence. The survivors stressed that family, friends, and congregants must educate themselves if they want to be partners with victims in addressing the issue.

They stated that although it may appear that resources and education may not seem to help or resolve the issue quickly, having the resources available helps greatly when victims are ready to confront the issue. They stated that validating victims and helping them build on their strengths is key for victims and families.

Validation and Building on Strengths

The survivors stated during the discussion that having a confidant to validate and build on their strengths was imperative in helping them survive the abuse. One survivor told a story of how her sister, who was very aware of the IPV issues, consistently validated her feelings regarding the situation. She reported that she spent many days and nights experiencing a wide spectrum of feelings as her husband abused her physically. The survivor confided in her sister that she still loved him very much and could not imagine leaving. She would tell her sister how her husband was under duress because the ministry was not flourishing as he expected and finances continued to fluctuate monthly. Her sister would constantly reinforce that her feelings and emotions were normal and encouraged her to take time to sort through the full range of her emotions before she made important decisions about when to leave.

The survivors stated that not having their feelings validated reinforces blame and self-deprecating behaviors that push victims into a hole of isolation, refusing to communicate and falling further into despair and depression. They stated that it is difficult to quickly separate from the man they married, birthed and nurtured children with, and built a life with around ministry and family despite abuse issues. They stated that to forsake everything they established without validating their feelings and emotions is comparable to removing a scab before the sore is healed.

The validation aspect is crucial, especially in the early stages of IPV, to help victims cope with the shock of the initial abuse, gain emotional stability, and develop an escape plan. The survivors discussed how supportive individuals understand the need to build on strengths to constantly reinforce positive behavior in decision making. The survivors stated that having someone to support their initial decision to stay with the abuser was enormous in terms allowing them to think on their own about the next steps to address the issue. They stated that most individuals, although they have good intentions, rarely understand the psychological impact of IPV and how this affects their lives on a daily basis. They stated that most individuals believe that victims are free to make and implement decisions on their own even when the abuser is not present.

One survivor stated that her sister had good intentions but lacked the skill set to help her address the IPV. She stated that her sister constantly told her what she needed to do instead of listening and supporting her thoughts about safety and protection. She stated that her sister acted in some respects like the abuser by dominating discussions and refusing to listen and encourage her during the process.

The survivors commented that it was important to experience small victories that provided strength and hope in the midst of daily encounters with abuse. They stated that taking these small steps in the direction of making phone calls for resources, talking with advocates, or packing important information in preparation for transition took immense courage, and validating survivors for taking these imperative steps proved to be very helpful for them. They stated that individuals fail to understand that each time victims make a decision to leave it literally means that they take a chance with their lives or the lives of their children.

They also discussed how they must be extremely careful in how they implement a process of transition and need individuals to understand their plight, build up their strengths, validate their emotions, constantly acknowledge small victories, and support their decision making process, even if they disagree.

5. What were some of the actions from people that were not helpful to you?

The survivors reiterated that individuals who displayed dominant behaviors in terms of directing them on how to deal with IPV were certainly not helpful in their transition to safety. They reiterated that although individuals desired to help, dominating behaviors caused them to shut down and withhold information, as they perceived them in the same light as the abusers. Directing victims stripped away their ability to think and take ownership of their transition processes, instead relying on another individual to validate their thoughts rather than treat them as the expert.

One survivor told of a confrontation she encountered with a friend in church who openly discussed her situation without mentioning her name in hopes that this would motivate her to contact law enforcement. She stated that eventually church members discovered the problem and how the circumstance escalated with her husband. He accepted another pastorate in a different state and continued with the abuse. The survivor stated that this made things worse as the family moved to a very small town, with only five thousand residents, which made it more difficult to address the issues as her husband became a respected pastor in the community by establishing relationships with law enforcement and politicians, serving as a volunteer chaplain and board member on various volunteer committees.

Further, many of the small town officials eventually became members of the church and considered him an upstanding civil servant, thus making it arduous to deal with the yelling and threatening behavior of her husband.

Misguided Faith

The survivors stated that it was not helpful when church members encouraged them to rely on help from God rather than using other means of intervention to address the issue. They stated that it became apparent that spirituality was not the answer as they discussed different options with confidants, friends, and family. One survivor told a story of how she disclosed the abuse to the local bishop and he suggested that she continue to seek the face of the Lord and pray that her husband would be delivered from the spirit of anger and control. The survivor stated that the bishop encouraged her to believe that God would turn the situation around and her husband would become the loving person she believed him to be while she continued to suffer daily. The survivor stated that she was told to believe God for a miracle and not leave her family destitute and helpless. The survivor commented that the action of the bishop was misguided and immensely inappropriate as he had no formal training to address IPV.

Prayer and Fasting

The survivors stated that the suggestion to pray and fast to cast the devil out of their husbands was not helpful in addressing the problem. They stated that at the end of the experience they understood that prayer and fasting were not actions that immediately helped them transition to safety. They confirmed that although prayer and fasting are necessary spiritual disciplines, they did not assist in the process of addressing abuse. The survivors stated that they grew weary of the recommendation to believe God through prayer, fasting, faith, and Scripture of how God would use them to bring deliverance to their husbands.

A few of the survivors commented that the worst aspect of misguided faith was a pastor or bishop suggesting that they speak with other women who had been abused who prayed and fasted and their husbands were miraculously delivered from abusing them and still serving God faithfully in the church. One survivor shared a story of how her confidant requested that they commit to daily prayer and fasting together and believe that God would touch her husband in a special way to open his eyes about his behavior, with the goal of him repenting of his sin and being reconciled to God and his wife. The survivor stated that she committed to prayer and fasting but the abuse grew worse once her husband discovered her intent of praying and fasting at the church with another person. The survivor stated that in retrospect she would have handled the process much differently.

Focus Group Interviews

Better Wife

The survivors agreed that another unhelpful action was the suggestion that if they would seek to become better wives, more supportive of their husband's ministry, and more faithful to the church, their husbands would relate to them better and have little inclination for IPV. They stated in some cases they were encouraged to be more pleasing and loving as a strategy to decrease the tension their husbands encountered with the demands of ministry and work. This form of blaming the wife to justify the husband's behavior pushed them further into depression, with virtually no hope to see light at the end of the tunnel.

The survivors stated that the action of blaming provided support for continued abuse by placing the blame in the wrong aspect of the relationship. The survivors stated that blaming led them to believe that they needed to become better wives and support their husbands to ease the burden at home, and if the abuse continued it was their fault. They implemented diverse methods to become better wives, which included becoming more spiritual and increasing interest in their husband's ministry work in lieu of pursuing their own callings and ministry gifts. They also stated that they perceived that becoming a better wife meant changing their approach and response to their husband by cooking his favorite dinner, looking more attractive, taking better care of the children at home, and creating an environment that reduced his level of anger.

One survivor told a story of how she did everything to become a better wife at the advice of a friend in hopes that her husband would no longer abuse. The survivor stated that the strategy backfired as her husband became suspicious of her behavior and began to question her to determine if she was sincere or attempting to transition to safety. There was another survivor who stated that her husband noticed the change in her behavior and conversation about becoming a better wife, and although the abuse decreased, this allowed him to delve into alternative activities such as Internet pornography and online dating, which led to an affair. The survivors stated that the advice of accepting blame and becoming a better wife was not helpful and in most cases increased the problem or created a pathway for their husbands to participate in other immoral activities.

Treat Him in This Manner

The survivors stated that another action that was not helpful was recommendations from individuals on exactly how to treat and support their husbands. They stated that this comes under the umbrella of becoming a better wife. They commented that advice on how they should interact and engage with their husbands was highly insensitive and perturbing. They stated that individuals lacked the discernment to understand victims, abuse, and the devastating impact on families. The survivors stated that individuals who provided preposterous suggestions were merely caught up in the man behind the pulpit preaching, teaching, praying for the sick, performing infant baptisms, and other pastoral duties. They failed to understand that the man behind the pulpit was an abusive, angry, and controlling person behind closed doors and damaged the lives of his family on a daily basis. The survivors stated that individuals must be extremely careful in their perceptions and understanding of another woman's husband and IPV, and not judge the person or circumstance too quickly.

6. What advice would you give to women today who encounter IPV?

Recognize the Warning Signs

The advice the survivors would give to women who encounter abuse is to quickly recognize the warning signs and symptoms before the situation escalates. They stated that in most cases women fall deeply in love and ignore the warning signs, especially in the event that the abuse is non-physical. The survivors commented that most women who experience the non-physical aspects of domestic violence fail to understand that it still falls under the umbrella of abuse.

Women will allow or permit elevated voices, intimidation, bullying tactics, economic control, and psychological abuse without understanding that those forms of abuse in some cases lead to physical abuse. The survivors stated that it is important for women to pay special attention to the patterns and behaviors of the non-physical characteristics during the courting period and refrain from looking the other way in the midst of infatuation, love, and marriage.

Focus Group Interviews

Be Aware of Their Fear

The survivors stated that women should not be afraid to seek assistance and immediately leave when they recognize signs and symptoms. They should not be afraid to talk to a friend or confidant who can help them analyze the situation and strategically construct a swift transition plan. They reaffirmed that fear is one of the most tantalizing weapons that abusers utilize to stifle women from thinking and preparing safety plans. The survivors commented that it is immensely difficult to overcome the initial and ongoing fear associated with domestic violence, but acknowledged that women who experience abuse must not allow fear to strip them of the ability to formulate a plan to flee. They stated that they would encourage women to embrace their inner strength to confront the issue of fear that most often times prevents and discourages reporting.

Practice Prevention

The survivors talked at length about recognizing the signs and symptoms of IPV early in the cycle to prevent the issue from becoming a much larger problem. They stated that most women wholeheartedly believe that their husbands will change through prayer, fasting, becoming a better wife, and taking a subservient position that allows their husbands to maintain dominance without resistance.

The survivors reaffirmed the danger of disregarding the early signs and symptoms and stated that they would advise women to seek assistance quickly to decrease the opportunity for abuse to overtake their lives. One survivor stated that her inner voice spoke loud and clear about the warning signs, but she married her fiancé in a lavish ceremony and then endured many years of IPV. The survivor stated that she regrets failing to address the issues that were in plain view early in the process.

She stated that women can ill afford to deliberate the signs; she commented that women must take immediate action to prohibit further issues that impact women and entire families. The survivors also stated that it is important for women to be fully aware of the Power and Control Wheel as well as the cycle of abuse, as both depict the abuser's strategy in gaining full control over a period of time. The survivors stated that awareness of the eclectic stages of IPV and methods abusers use provide women with the tools and resources necessary to minimize intensification in the early stages.

One survivor commented that awareness and education saved her from experiencing long-term issues in her marriage as compared to another woman she knew in her church. The survivor stated that the training she obtained at her church prior to marrying her husband was essential in discontinuing IPV for any long period of time. She stated that through awareness she was able to identify the signs early and escape the abuse.

Educating People

The survivors overwhelmingly stated that the lack of education was one of the most prevalent factors in ongoing cases of IPV. They stated that they would advise any woman to obtain some type of education about abuse by attending seminars, training, and conferences to gain a full understanding of the issue. The survivors stated that most women in the church have no clue about the nature of abuse and fail to possess the knowledge to escape abusive situations. Most pastor's wives do not believe that their husbands possess the attitude to initiate domestic violence because they preach God's word and therefore are not susceptible to commit such heinous acts of violence against women.

They stated that the church is the perfect environment for men to parade their love for God and the church while abusing their wives under the nose of the most spiritual Christians in the church. The survivors stated that they would advise women to educate themselves prior to any courtship, proposal, or engagement leading to marriage. The survivors stated that once the marriage is consummated it is almost too late for many women to avoid IPV, and it is arduous to begin an education process once the abuse has begun. Embracing some form of training would give women the opportunity to escape domestic violence. The survivors stated that they would also advise women to educate themselves during their single years and would also advise pastors and ministry leadership teams to provide educational opportunities in youth settings, starting at the elementary stage, continuing through college and well into adulthood. They stated that it is essential for young girls and women to be able to comprehend the signs and symptoms of abuse and be able to recognize the behaviors and patterns of abusive men.

Focus Group Interviews

Understanding What God Says

The survivors commented that women should take additional time to obtain a biblical understanding of marriage and the roles of husbands and wives. They stated that most women in the church lack the understanding of these roles and the issue of IPV is almost never discussed in any length during premarital counseling, especially from a theological perspective. The survivors stated that they would advise women to attend a seminary or locate a ministry that can assist them with obtaining a correct biblical view on marriage and spousal roles. They commented that having this understanding of Scripture will help women recognize when the roles are blurred and what to expect from a potential husband during the course of marriage.

This will also equip women to deal with the potential trap of remaining in abusive marriages because of an incorrect interpretation of Scripture. The survivors would encourage women to present questions to pastors and church leaders to gain an understanding of how the ministry views marriage, IPV, femininity, and marriage roles. They stated that most women in the Black church simply trust the words of the pastor and church leadership as a result of how they were reared in church and family life. Most African Americans are taught to obey and not question the pastor to avoid punishment for disobedience and lack of faith in his words. The survivors stated that although more pastors have received training about IPV in the Black church and enrolled into seminary, the process for addressing the issue from a pastoral perspective needs much improvement in order to help women decrease the chances of marrying an abuser or remaining in an abusive relationship.

They commented that more pastors must shift their mindset and promote the message of domestic abuse from the pulpit to help victims overcome abuse and increase reporting.

Conclusion

The focus group provided some great insights into the world of victims through their lens regarding the impact of IPV on the family. The experiences shared by these brave and courageous women highlight abuse and help us understand the mindset of abusers and victims. The stories shared by these women confirm the responsibility of pastors and the church to protect women and encourage reporting. Christendom must understand the issue through the eyes of victims to grasp the full effect in an effort to provide helpful assistance and prevent the escalation of abuse.

The church must be cognizant of the reasons why many victims fail to report abuse and understand that it usually takes at least seven to nine occurrences before they report or attempt to leave. Further, it is important for Christians to comprehend the impact of abuse on families, especially when individuals take it upon themselves to act in the best interest of victims without their permission. This can quickly escalate the issue and cause more harm to victims and families. The church must be aware of their role in providing assistance to victims and families who experience domestic abuse. The actions of the church are critical, whether positive or negative, and can have an immense impact on the ability of victims to transition into safety. Active listening is the most essential tool in helping victims develop plans to address their circumstance. The survivors overwhelmingly stated that some friends and confidants attempted to fulfill the role of subject matter expert, but lacked the training to be effective in their approach.

Lastly, survivors reiterated that women must recognize the signs and symptoms early and educate themselves during their single years to obtain a better chance of having an abuse-free marriage.

Chapter 5

IPV Prevention in the Black Church

THE BLACK CHURCH IS poised to enhance its methodology for addressing IPV against women. The previous chapter illustrated the devastating impact of abuse against women as they shared their personal experiences with domestic violence. The women suffered unimaginable abuse, some for longer periods of time than others, enduring the pain and agony of coping with family and marital issues in multiple forms. The arduous experiences of these women demonstrate the need for enhanced prevention efforts by the church not only to reduce the occurrences of abuse, but more importantly to help women report. The experiences of the women in chapter 4 underscore the need for the church to develop internal policies through the creation of a human resources department where staff, volunteers, and congregants can report abuse to a separate entity within the church to combat domestic violence and underreporting.

The thesis of this writing centers on the victimization of women and their hesitation to report IPV. Prevention in the church must start with encouraging women to report to church officials or law enforcement, especially when abuse occurs in the presence of children. Christendom must continue its education and awareness about violence against women and progress to the next steps of training coupled with the implementation of policies that hold abusers accountable, while protecting victims in the process. The church must incorporate a model of reporting abuse gleaned from government, education, and social services to aid women in coming forward. Christendom should embrace a new model of helping victims, inclusive of collaboration with advocates, to assist women who report with services that help protect women and children from ongoing abuse.

Historically, the Black church has been the center of the Black community and one of the few places where people could meet to strategize and develop plans to fight for justice and equality against the cruel effects of oppression, racism, and prejudice.[1] The Black church must begin to utilize the most powerful position in the church, the pulpit, as a place to advocate a zero tolerance policy against IPV. The pulpit was the place of power for the galvanization of Blacks during slavery, Jim Crow, and the Civil Rights Movement. The spoken word from the pulpit proved to be a source of power, hope, and comfort; so the spoken word must again become a source of justice for victims of violence in our pulpits today.

The church has always been a place of empowerment, providing Blacks with the courage to challenge the dominant forces of White slave masters and government to gain freedom that would ring loud like the liberty bell in the city of brotherly love.[2] Today, the church faces perhaps a greater challenge in providing services for victims, utilizing the pulpit—as in times past—as the place to galvanize pastors and leaders to decry the distressing effects of abuse, walking hand in hand with advocates to lift the plight of women, sending a strong message to abusers that violence against women is prohibited.[3] The spoken word is the key to reducing abuse by empowering women to report.

The hallmark of encouraging women to report begins with training and educating pastors and leaders on the impact of abuse, using the previous four chapters as a framework to assist in understanding the issue of abuse, the historical origins, the theological underpinnings, and stories from survivors with a focus on reporting. The church must realize that IPV has two sides, the spiritual and secular. Although this section will not delve into an understanding of both sides, the focus will center on a methodology for collaboration. Christendom cannot address the issue alone through the use of Scripture, prayer, and fasting; this has to be combined with collective efforts of law enforcement, the legal community, hospitals, and government to provide services to victims and families and bring accountability to the abusers. The church must evolve into one of the leading entities that directly challenges the stereotypes and myths regarding victims of domestic violence by providing innovative services to protect women and help them report.

1. Belk, "On Sunday, Faith, and Freedom."
2. Moore, "African-American Church."
3. Black, "Role of the Black Church in Addressing IPV."

Women's Hesitance to Report IPV

In chapter 4, the survivors overwhelmingly confirmed their fear to report IPV for three reasons. First, *they feared that their lives and the lives of their children would be in danger if they attempted to escape.* Second, *reporting to pastors and church officials accomplished nothing and in most cases added to the duress of the circumstance and incited revenge against them for reporting.* Third, *there was a lack of understanding among law enforcement, pastors, and church officials concerning abuse.* Christendom must respond with vigilance to assist women in the church who experience abuse and increase opportunities for women to report.

The Black church must be willing to alter its perspective, examine diverse models of reporting, and embed a reporting model within the internal policies of the church bylaws and human resources handbook. Further, as previously stated, the church must collaborate with a wide array of advocates in the community to extend services and resources to women and children. The response must be extensive and robust from the most powerful position in the church, the pulpit, and the most powerful person in the church, the pastor. The goal is to create an environment of deterrence of abuse and empower of women to report.

Protocol for Reporting IPV in the Black Church

The Black church has a long history of suppressing reports of IPV as well as discouraging women from reporting abuse. We must take this great opportunity to develop a protocol that empowers women to report, which is essential in reducing abuse in the church and increase prevention efforts. Although there is some level of awareness regarding domestic violence against women, the church must increase its attentiveness to the problem and introduce several strategies to reduce abuse against women. This will be accomplished in two phases. In the first phase, the church must develop a reporting requirement and embed it into the internal policies of the church bylaws through training, education, and awareness. Secondly, through building a strong network of advocates and community experts, the church must provide immediate and ongoing services to victims and survivors. This two-pronged approach is the substratum for the church to develop a model to address the issue of abuse against women in the church. The church must analyze the various models of reporting from public and private entities in order to develop an internal model congregants can use to report.

Models of Reporting

Churches are in a great position to create a reporting system to help address IPV and reduce the length of time women remain in abusive relationships. Although national data states that it takes seven to nine instances of abuse before a woman seeks help,[4] it is imperative to note that most women continue in abusive relationships due to a limited understanding of and access to resources to escape abuse. This is exacerbated by the fact that most parishioners are not aware of the depth of the issue and receive little training about the signs and symptoms of abuse in the church and community. The church must establish reporting requirements within the ministry comprised of individuals who are mandated to report domestic abuse in the same manner as most social service professionals are mandated to report child abuse and neglect. The United States, Canada, Australia, and Europe have mandatory reporting laws for professionals who have regular contact with the most vulnerable members of society, namely seniors, the disabled, and children.[5] Mandatory reporters are required to report cases of abuse they directly observe or where abuse is suspected. Contingent upon individual states and respective laws, mandatory reporters are required to report cases of financial, physical, sexual, neglectful, and other types of abuse.[6] In 1962 two doctors, Henry Kempe and Brandt Steele, published "The Battered Child Syndrome" to assist doctors in recognizing child abuse and establishing requirements to report abuse to authorities.[7]

Subsequently, in 1974 the United States Congress passed the Child Abuse Prevention and Treatment Act (CAPTA), which provided funding to states to develop Child Protection Services (CPS) departments and reporting hotlines to combat serious injuries to children. Although CAPTA was specific to physical abuse, reporting abuse evolved into the reporting of sexual abuse and emotional abuse, as well as neglect, bruises, abuse of the developmentally delayed, psychological abuse, and exposure to IPV.[8]

4. Alabama Coalition Against Domestic Violence, "Barriers to Leaving."
5. Mathews, "Mandatory Reporting Legislation."
6 Besharov, "Doing Something About Child Abuse."
7. Kempe and Helfer, eds., *Battered Child*, 35–45.
8. Krason, "Critics of Current Child Abuse Laws ."

Mandatory reporters are required to report actual or suspected cases of abuse whether they are in paid, unpaid, or voluntary positions, as well as abuse committed by child care providers, adult care providers, and elder care providers.[9]

State of Oregon Mandatory Reporting

The state of Oregon requires that any private or public official having reasonable cause to believe that any child they come in contact with has experienced some type of abuse is required to immediately report. Public and private individuals who are required to report include doctors, law enforcement, government employees, legislators, educators, clergy, therapists, hospital staff, and practitioners, per the Child Abuse Act.[10] The state of Oregon has a model of reporting in which mandatory reporters contact a child abuse hotline and file a confidential report of abuse. The confidential report is taken by a child abuse hotline employee, who conducts research to determine if there were previous reports of abuse.

A report can also be made in writing or through the agency website. If the employee determines that there were no previous reports of abuse and the information presented does not meet the criteria of abuse, the case is considered unsubstantiated and closed. If there is sufficient evidence that abuse has occurred or is suspected, a referral is made to a local office for a CPS worker to follow up within twenty-four hours to conduct a home visit, interview of all parties involved, and a written assessment that will outline whether the case was substantiated or unsubstantiated upon the initial investigation. If the claim of abuse is unsubstantiated, then the case is closed. If the claim of abuse is substantiated, the next steps involve CPS workers making the difficult decision to remove the child from the home with placement in temporary foster care or recommend that the child remain in the home and provide services to the family. If the child is removed from the home and placed in temporary foster care, the case of removal is presented before a judge, who determines whether the removal is justified and the child should remain in temporary foster care, or the child should

---

9. https://www.childwelfare.gov.
10. Oregon Department of Human Services, "Mandatory Reporting."

remain in the home, or a combination of the two.[11] All fifty states in the U.S. have mandatory laws for reporting child abuse and neglect.[12]

DuPage County School District, Illinois

The DuPage County School District established a policy to address the reporting of child abuse and neglect that requires all school personnel to report per the Child Abuse Act. The policy states that all school personnel must contact the Children and Family Services (CFS) hotline when they have reasonable cause to suspect that a minor has been abused or neglected or is in danger of being abused and neglected. After the phone call has been made to CFS, an investigation will be conducted to determine the accuracy of the report and the next steps to protect the child in collaboration with law enforcement. Mandatory reporters who fail to make a good faith effort to report abuse may be subject to prosecution, license suspension, and civil liability.[13]

Clergy as Mandatory Reporters

In many states clergy, per state statute, are designated as mandatory reporters of child abuse and neglect. As of November 2013, there were twenty-seven states that specified clergy as mandatory reporters.[14] In the states of Delaware, Florida, Idaho, Kentucky, Maryland, Utah, and Wyoming, where clergy are not considered mandatory reporters, they may be included in the "any person" category of those required to report.[15] Furthermore, not all states allow confidentiality of pastor communications or clergy-penitent privilege in which communication remains confidential. The privilege of confidentiality varies from state to state and clergy must be cognizant of the laws regarding clergy-penitent privilege.[16] The church should be encouraged to follow the model of reporting as outlined above for local, regional,

11. Oregon Department of Human Services, "Child Abuse and Neglect Reporting Numbers."

12. National Center for Prosecution of Child Abuse, "Mandatory Reporting of Child Abuse and Neglect."

13. DuPage County, "Model Policy."

14. Child Welfare Information Gateway, "Clergy as Mandatory Reporters."

15. Ibid.

16. Ibid.

and national agencies. Christendom must ensure that clergy understand that they are mandated in some states to report child abuse and IPV that occurs in the presence of children.

The Christian church must develop internal ministry protocols and policies that require church officials to report domestic abuse in the same manner that child abuse is reported, even though reporting domestic violence is not required by law unless it occurs in the presence of a minor child.

Theological Mandate for Reporting

The mandate to report should be a part of the initial training for pastors and church leaders. The mandate for reporting abuse falls under the framework of a theological mandate based in Scripture. The proverbial writer states in Proverbs 21:13 that if an individual shuts their ears to the cry of the poor their own cry will not be heard. Church leaders must fully embrace the theological mandate for reporting abuse and protecting victims. This is imperative, as the husbands of the eight women interviewed in chapter 4 were clergy or leaders in the church. Church officials must keep their ears open to hear the cry of the abused and oppressed and not divert the marginalized to the spiritual disciplines of prayer, fasting, and devotion as a methodology to assist victims.

The Leviticus writer warned the children of Israel to refrain from sacrificing their children through the fire of Moloch. Moloch was a Canaanite god that was offered the sacrifices of children by their parents among the Canaanites and Phoenicians.[17] Although this may be perceived as a difficult comparison to victims of abuse, pastors and church leaders must comprehend that if they shut their ears to the cry of the abused and oppressed, they assist in the process of sacrificing the health and well-being of victims and children to the fire of domestic violence.

The Black church must place a greater emphasis on reporting firsthand incidents of IPV in the same manner as child abuse and neglect. Although there are no state or federal laws that require clergy or community members to report domestic violence, unless it occurs in the presence of children, the church and community must be strongly encouraged to follow the Good Samaritan principal and report occurrences of abuse even when children are not present. This is a gray area for the church as the secular community continues to struggle with the development of mandatory

---

17. Milgrom, *Leviticus*, 197–200.

reporting laws for violence. The church and secular communities are both comprised of humans whose hearts must remain compassionate, and the theological mandate to report incidents of IPV must become central even when children are not present.

IPV Awareness

The information provided throughout the book is important in developing a framework for the mandatory reporting of domestic abuse in the Black church. The model for reporting should begin with a solid definition of IPV, such as how its defined in the first chapter. The definition will be the catalyst to launch the "Awareness Campaign" directly from the pulpit, with the pastor serving as the chief ambassador and campaign chairperson with a strong message of awareness and education about domestic violence. The Black church has a strong tradition of oral history, particularly in the call and response methodology that exists between the pastor and congregation. The congregation adheres to the instructions and direction of the pastor and this can be powerful in the campaign to help women report abuse in the church. The pastor must seize the opportunity to utilize the power and influence of his voice to raise and sustain congregational awareness in order to embed IPV awareness into the culture of the church.

Embedding IPV into church culture is immensely important to preventing abuse from being labeled as a seasonal topic during the month of October (Domestic Violence Awareness Month) or when high-profile incidents occur among athletes or celebrities. The pastor must take the lead position, along with the leadership team, to actively participate in awareness events, promoting healthy relationships, marriages, and family while standing strong against family violence. The Black church must allow innovation to assist in the creation of domestic violence awareness events and activities such as Stomp the Silence, Stop the Violence in Mississippi; Surviving Domestic Violence in California; the Seminole County Domestic Violence Vigil in Florida; and Marital Bliss: Couples Date Night in Virginia.[18]

The church must glean from these events and propose robust activities to raise and sustain awareness. For example, the Black church has a rich history of food and fellowship that can be utilized to draw congregants together for discussion forums, seminars, and a remembrance and

18. National Resource Center on Domestic Violence, "DVAM Events."

celebration event to reflect on the stories of survivors. The church must implement similar activities to embed awareness within the culture of the church and congregation and no longer casually discuss the issue of IPV. The followers of the kingdom must tear down the walls of silence and bring the issue to the forefront of the church starting in the pulpit. The stigmas that stifle women in the Black church from reporting must be totally shattered to allow women the freedom to report abuse or seek a safe space to discuss safety plans and escape strategies.

IPV Education

The educational aspect is immensely important in prevention and helping congregants comprehend the perennial effects of abuse. Education helps to remove the plethora of myths and misinformation about IPV that support silence and secrecy to prevail. The Black church is primed to offer a robust educational campaign that inculcates parishioners and transcends beyond the first step of awareness. The educational campaign is the second step in the prevention process. Christendom must create a framework for educating congregants and should begin with a survey to measure the IPV educational baseline of the congregation to assess the level of knowledge among parishioners. The next step in the educational process centers on the development of training material to educate the church about IPV. This is imperative as some congregants may arrive at the training session with preconceived notions based upon cultural, religious, and self-imposed comprehension. The educational training can also be demarcated based upon the level of understanding of each congregant or parishioner group. The education sessions could be separated based on the results of the individual survey in the following manner: introductory level, intermediate level, experienced level, and advocate level.

The Introductory Level

The introductory level would assist congregants with understanding the working definition of IPV, the signs and symptoms of IPV, the cycle of abuse, the Power and Control Wheel, and other basic information. The introductory session would also include a moment for congregants to reflect on how abuse has impacted their lives directly or indirectly, discussion in small groups, question and answers, and post-training follow-up sessions.

The question-and-answer sessions for the introductory level are crucial to build a solid foundation for congregants who have little to no awareness of domestic violence issues. In the introductory level, congregants would be introduced to local agencies that provide services for victims and survivors.

The Intermediate Level

The intermediate level would consist of a review of the basic comprehension of IPV, delve into the specifics of the signs and symptoms, and include an in-depth breakdown of the cycle of abuse and the Power and Control Wheel. The intermediate level would also learn about the struggles of victims in deciding to leave, reasons why they stay, and an introduction into the mind of abusers. This level would include self-reflection of the impact of IPV directly or indirectly on individuals' lives in small group discussions and question-and-answer sessions. The intermediate level is equally important as the introductory level to continue the overall education of congregants by providing more in-depth education and increasing the ability of congregants to intervene in certain circumstances.

The Experienced Level

The experienced level would begin with a basic knowledge test of IPV, the cycle of abuse, the Power and Control Wheel, the signs and symptoms of IPV, and the impact of abuse on children and family life. At the experienced level, an agency advocate will be present and congregants will learn about resources, how advocates work to help victims, and how we can work with them.

The Advocate Level

The advocate level is the substratum for training, and the goal for all congregants as this level is the pinnacle for prevention in the church. The first three levels of educational training are important components to the advocate level as the step to help significantly reduce violence against women in the church. The advocate level will consist of a "train the trainer" framework in which advocates are trained to provide assistance to congregants in the first three levels and serve as resident experts and consultants for the church and ministry. The advocates would be responsible for conducting quarterly or semi-annual training, education, and awareness inclusive of the latest trends in IPV. Although every parishioner will not attain this desired level, the pastor and church ministry leaders would be strongly encouraged to reach this level. At this level, advocates will teach why victims experience what they do, and why batterers are controlling as well as an introduction to some of the legal issues victims encounter. It is important that pastors and leadership teams on all levels continue to support victims to report, create safe spaces for discussion and consultation, and help reduce incidents through vigorous training and education. The advocates would be strongly encouraged to attend some type of advanced training and attend a national or regional conference yearly as a type of continuing education credit to stay abreast on the latest IPV trends.

The awareness campaign, education, and training at the introductory, intermediate, experienced, and advocate levels are essential for the church to launch an aggressive internal campaign from the pulpit to raise awareness and encourage women to report abuse. The Black church must take the lead in the faith-based community by taking a strong stance against domestic abuse and develop a reporting system for church officials that offer victims a safe space for listening and consultation. This can be accomplished by ensuring that churches create a human resource department that aids the ministerial and leadership staff in the development of internal policies that help embed awareness and encourage reporting.

The notion of policy development through an HR department can assist in embedding awareness in the ministry culture and hold paid and volunteer staff accountable for addressing and reporting domestic abuse as they become aware of issues. Although there is no state or federal law that requires individuals to report IPV, except in the presence of children, the church must invoke the theological mandate of reporting to protect victims and encourage victims to report in the same manner that child abuse and neglect is reported. However, the focus must be on the issue of the lack of power, vulnerability, and lack of control that victims experience at the hands of those in positions of power. Victims of IPV will continue to suffer as long as the issue remains at a non-mandatory reporting level.

Internal Policy Development

The state of Oregon, as well as many other U.S. states, have internal policies housed in local and state agencies that provide guidance to staff and volunteers who assist victims of IPV. The model that will be utilized in this section of the writing will focus on the Oregon Department of Human Services (DHS) and Human Resources Department (HR) to assist the Black church in creating a policy and guideline for churches to follow when reports of abuse are received.

The development of an internal policy is critical in helping victims report abuse as well as the development of safe spaces to tell their story, construct safety plans, and request assistance for relocation, especially for children. Although it is a daunting task for churches and ministries to develop internal policies, it is equally daunting to handle domestic violence issues in the same manner they always have. This has left many victims abused and unprotected, and children exposed to psychological and sociological harm. The church must now be poised to transition from awareness, education, and training into effective internal policy development.

Pastoral Care Departments—IPV Focused

The development of a pastoral care department that is specific to addressing IPV within the context of church ministry is not a new process, as more church ministries continue to hire full-time paid staff to lead ministry departments such as music, praise and worship, education and schools, youth and young adults, as well as men's and women's ministries. The pastoral care department would function in similar fashion to a secular human resources department.

The HR department for the state of Oregon is specific to each state agency but similar in scope and responsibility in guiding managers and employees. The HR department handles issues of employee discipline, termination, roles and responsibilities of all employees, core values, professional interactions between employees, and background checks for all employees. Full-time staff that are hired agree to a criminal, child abuse, and elder abuse background check that they must successfully pass in order to be hired, especially when employment involves providing services to Oregon's most vulnerable citizens.

Many HR departments in state government are now mandated by federal and state law to provide assistance for employees who are victims of IPV and stalking. This is inclusive of assisting employees with relocation efforts to different offices; changing the employee's name on the staff roster; providing other agency staff with the employee's name only on a need-to-know basis; and approving time off work to obtain restraining orders, attend court, and meet with lawyers, counselors, and advocates for ongoing assistance with abuse. The state of Oregon also offers a program for clients who desire to address IPV issues.

Temporary Assistance for Domestic Violence Survivors

The state of Oregon has a program entitled Temporary Assistance for Domestic Violence Survivors (TA-DVS) administered by case work staff who determine eligibility for the program, provide financial and non-financial assistance to eligible clients, and broker for services with community partners to help victims obtain needed assistance, including relocation efforts. The term *client* refers to an individual who applies for the program and is in need of assistance.

The program is housed under the umbrella program of Temporary Assistance for Needy Families (TANF) program, which provides temporary financial assistance to eligible families with children as adults seek services to become self-sufficient. The TA-DVS program starts with an individual making a request and completing an application. Once the application is received and screened, an appointment is made with case work staff to determine eligibility and discuss next steps. The victim is not required to provide proof or file for a restraining order, a no contact order, or police report. The victim's story and care of a minor child are the only proof needed to apply and be eligible for services.

The crux of the TA-DVS program involves case management services to assist victims by creating a safety plan developed jointly by the client and case worker for protection, safety, and employment. The goal at this juncture is not to explore all of the eligibility requirements, but to discuss how to create a safety plan and provide services and resources for victims and families to be used as a model and guide for the pastoral care department in the church. The TA-DVS program may provide assistance to victims in the form of payments for motels and safe places in undisclosed locations away from the abuser. The program also has limited funding to relocate victims and families to undisclosed locations out of state via airplane, train, bus, or by providing gas vouchers for those who choose to drive to an undisclosed location. These options are part of the safety plan for victims and families. The program also works in conjunction with the Oregon Department of Justice to provide a confidential address and phone numbers, or identity protection.

The pastoral care department must also develop internal policies for abuse victims, especially if they are an employee or member of the church. The policies must be inclusive of specific actions that occur when issues have been discovered or reported. The policy must consist of the following components: the definition of IPV; reporting requirements for pastors, associate ministers, ministry leaders, and volunteers; methodology for reporting; how assistance will be provided for abuse victims; how to report domestic violence in the presence of children; a specific policy for staff and volunteers who are victims of family violence; and a specific policy for members that are unpaid staff or volunteers.

Development of a Pastoral Care Department to Address IPV

The pastoral care department in the church must be encouraged to review TA-DVS program and seek ways to implement portions of the program to provide assistance to congregants in need of help. The church must invoke a new prototype that embraces a new vision of how to aid victims and families. The past methods of prayer, fasting, Bible study, blame, shame, and silence have discouraged victims from reporting and encouraged them to continue in abusive relationships. This antiquated system must be exchanged for the creation of a pastoral care department that mirrors the model above and helps victims. However, the criterion of having a minor child should not be required as in the TA-DVS program. The policy within the pastoral care department can simply state that congregants who are victims of abuse can require when they report IPV to a pastor or church official, the request is forwarded to the pastoral care department to address with the victim. This is immensely imperative if the abuser attends the same church as the victim.

The pastoral care department would function as an independent entity to investigate reports specifically when the incident is between a husband and wife or between significant others. This removes the investigation and decision making from the hands of the pastor, ministerial team, or church officials, who in the past have protected abusers and left victims helpless, encouraging them to remain in or return to abusive relationships. The pastoral care department should be the sole entity responsible for assisting women, investigating reports of abuse, and helping to resolve conflicts in cases of reconciliation. They should refer couples to neutral entities for family and individual therapy and counseling, develop strategic safety plans, and assist in the relocation of congregants for safety if necessary. The role of the pastor and church officials is immensely important, specifically around financial assistance, as the pastoral care department typically does not handle financial matters. They would work in conjunction with the finance committee and pastoral team as well as broker for services with local IPV advocate groups to provide services to victims. Having this internal process for congregants is vital for helping victims report abuse.

The process must be inclusive of presenting the pastoral care department with a restraining order or no contact order naming the abuser and associates as a deterrent against abusers and associates. They would be prohibited from entering the property; law enforcement would be notified of a violation of the order, and they would be removed from all church property. The next option to assist an individual who desires to remain at the same church is a possible change of identity as a preventative measure to misdirect the abuser or associates of the whereabouts of the victim and assist victims with relocation to a different church.

The Black church should embrace the concept of assisting women in the ministry with employment retention, safety, and protection. For example, in the COGIC church there are thousands of congregations in the U.S. and worldwide where pastoral care departments, working in conjunction with the local pastor, district superintendent, and jurisdictional bishops, can relocate a congregant who requests a transfer due to ongoing or unresolved IPV issues.

The pastoral care department in the church is encouraged embrace this policy for congregants who experience IPV and are in need of assistance. The paradigm must shift away from sending the victim to one corner and the abuser to the other corner in hopes that through prayer and fasting the abuser "sees the light" and the victim has a "spirit of forgiveness," thus encouraging the victim to reconcile with an abuser and start with a clean slate. The Christian church should be strongly encouraged to create pastoral care departments to specifically address abuse with qualified experts who are able to assist victims and families with resources to address domestic violence.

The establishment of an independent pastoral care department will hopefully encourage more women to report and provide hope that the report will not be swept under the rug of silence and pushed to the back burner of secrecy. The pastoral care department must be granted authority to investigate reports of abuse, even if a report is made against the pastor. The process will provide fairness, safety, and protection for victims, but more importantly will encourage more women to report regardless of the position, power, and authority of the abuser. The awareness campaign, education, training, policy development, and establishment of an independent pastoral care department are crucial to prevention and essential in encouraging women to report.

The pastoral care department would also consist of individuals with the title of "shepherding teams" of church elders, church leaders, and married couples who provide support to victims and families. The notion of policy development assists greatly in embedding IPV prevention in the culture of the church and ministry. The next step to further embed domestic violence awareness into the culture is taking the protocols developed and embedding them into the bylaws of the church.

Embedding IPV Policy within the Church Bylaws

The bylaws of any church serve as the organization's operating rules. The federal government does not require specific language although some states may require certain language. In Oregon, non-profit organizations, specifically religious organizations, are mandated to have certain language in the articles of incorporation that includes basic information such as name of the president, vice president, secretary, board members, and place of worship. More importantly, religious organizations are required to explain the process for the dissemination of assets upon dissolution, as the laws are clear that no one person can profit from a non-profit organization. The bylaws and articles of incorporation serve as the main deterrent for individuals who seek to profit from a non-profit organization.

The bylaws are the main document that binds all church members to the operating rules and procedures that cannot be superseded by any member of the church, not even the pastor. The bylaws are the single most powerful body of words to a church, second only to the Bible. The church bylaws generally are composed of separate articles that outline the operation of a particular function in the church.

For example, articles can state the principle and primary place of worship, the dissolution of assets, the qualifications of ministers and leaders, the roles of board members and trustees, the times and places of board meetings, etc. If an issue arises in the church that cannot be resolved by the members and results in litigation, the judge will not request a copy of the Bible; the judge will request a copy of the church bylaws to make a ruling.

The Black church must shape a new pattern for Christendom to follow utilizing the bylaws to further embed IPV within church culture. The bylaws must be the vehicle that cements awareness in a document that cannot be altered by the pastor, HR department, board of directors, trustees, or any member of the church. The bylaws are vital in aiding women in the church to shake the chains of silence and encourage them to report abuse in the church.

The key aspect to the bylaws resides in the fact that although a committee may develop and construct them, the entire church body must approve and adopt them by a two-thirds majority vote of members present. This is crucial, as all members of the congregation have a voice and, more importantly, a vote. Although the politics of persuasion can play a role in swaying the votes of members, all eligible voting parishioners play a vital role in the approval process. The Black church must take the next step to institutionalize IPV awareness into the culture of the church by strategically constructing explicit language regarding the impact of abuse and outlining a process to address domestic violence when it has been reported to church officials. The bylaws must specifically outline the process for investigating reports of IPV, including confidentiality, decision making, and the roles of the HR department, the pastor, the financial committee, associate ministers, and community partners.

The necessity of outlining the roles of each entity is critical to remove the threat of the most powerful position, the pastor, from overinvolvement in the process. The message must be embedded in the chief document of the church to raise the bar for other ministries while increasing opportunities for women to report. The church must sustain the internal policy development process, but also develop an external process to work in collaboration with non-religious NGOs to assist women in addressing family abuse issues.

The Black church is also poised to begin the process of establishing relationships with the IPV community to address the broader issues of abuse. The Christian church has mastered the ability to form relationships when addressing issues of civil rights, racism, prejudice, and poverty, but lacks strong partnerships with advocate communities to reduce domestic violence in the church and community. The internal and external process must join together to provide the greatest level assistance for victims.

The External Process: Community Collaboration

Christendom can ill afford to act in isolation, disconnected from the broader community, to resolve IPV issues using spiritual disciplines alone. The church can no longer address domestic abuse "in house" especially when it occurs in the presence of minor children, sweeping the problem under the carpet of silence and secrecy to protect men and exploit women. Although the Black Christian community generally mistrusts external intervention for theological reasons, the time is now for the church to stretch beyond its sealed walls and marble pulpits to lock hands with the community and provide assistance for victims. The external process for assisting victims must begin with disciples gaining awareness about organizations in the community that provide services to victims of IPV.

The awareness of the church should extend beyond the local church community and rise to the state and federal level to keep pastors and church leaders abreast of the most current trends in prevention and effective partnerships. The Black church must place prevention on the same platform as civil rights and work diligently to protect abused women. The external process is what I will refer to as the establishment of the fence approach. The fence approach is designed to place women in the middle of available services and build a fence of resources, advocates, and community partners that will assist women and help them report. The fence approach is modeled after the fence that home owners erect around their homes to prevent animals and humans from freely walking through their property and causing damage. The most important aspect of the house fence is to prevent children from the dangers of running into oncoming traffic. The Black church must be one of the fence planks that protect women from the horrors of abuse and provide safe spaces as they access other fence planks (community partners) to assist in reporting or escape. Christendom must embrace the fence approach by establishing fence planks within the broader IPV community that builds a fence around women who encounter abuse issues.

Building the Fence

The Black church, as previously stated, must embrace the fence approach by developing relationships with IPV advocates to extend the level of support and available resources for victims. For example, in the state of Oregon anyone can place a call to the 211 resource line and request information about IPV services. Domestic violence resources and services can be accessed through the following agencies: the American Bar Association Commission on Domestic and Sexual Assault, the Asian and Pacific Islander Institute on Domestic Violence, the Battered Women's Justice Project, Futures without Violence, Incite! Women of Color Against Domestic Violence, the National Center on Domestic and Sexual Violence, the National Coalition Against Domestic Violence, the Rave Project, the Faith Institute, and V-Day. These organizations provide a litany of services for individuals who need help reporting or escaping IPV. The fence should be constructed of diverse materials that play a critical role and support the overall goal of protecting women from abuse, power, control, and oppression. Christendom must be willing to build the fence of resources around women in the church who experience issues with domestic violence and ensure that these resources are available for victims.

The fence approach can be one of the most powerful coalitions that Christians can help develop to fight against IPV and increase opportunities for information to be disseminated into the community, which in turn will increase reporting. The fence can assist women in the church to break the tentacles of fear that hinder reporting and transition them to a place in which they are not only confident to report, but recognize the signs and symptoms and avoid abusive relationships altogether. The Black church must combine spiritual disciplines with the fence approach to provide a holistic approach in IPV prevention. Spiritual support must be married with fence support to assist women in accessing available resources from the spiritual community and IPV community. The task for Christians is to expand their reach to form fence planks to help women report and flee abuse. The IPV community is primed and ready to join with the faith-based community, placing religious and philosophical differences aside to work for the betterment of women in the church to report abuse.

Conclusion

THE STORY OF FIRST Lady B. and the survivors in chapter 4 serve as the voice for many women in the church and resonate with congregants impacted by IPV. There are many stories immensely similar to First Lady B. that are yet to be heard, as victims remain fearful to report abuse. The Black church, as well as all of Christendom, must recognize the significance and vastness of the issue, and no longer pretend that the problem is overemphasized by the media, journalist, and IPV advocates. The perennial issue of the fear to report domestic violence in the Black church continues to impede the necessary progress that is vital to significantly reducing abuse and non-reporting. The hesitancy to report is twofold in nature. First, *women are terrified to report out of fear of receiving more abuse, suffering injury, or even a fatality if their husbands find out they have reported.* Secondly, *women have the notion that reporting IPV to the pastor or church officials will place them and their families in greater risk of imminent danger.* This is further exacerbated when the abuser has an influential position in the church, specifically as the senior pastor.

The Christian church must tear down the bars of iron and walls of fear that protect abusers in the church and contribute to the perpetual victimization of women. Further, it is imperative that Black congregations understand the historical underpinnings of abuse in the church, beginning with their own church history as well as the historical perspective of slaves in the U.S. This is important as the church seeks to discover solutions to help victims and increase reporting. Christians must refrain from overspiritualizing IPV, burying the issue in the cemetery of prayer, fasting, Bible study, and spiritual disciplines.

Conclusion

The Black Pentecostal church must be encouraged to embrace education, training, and policy development with the goal of understanding how to serve women impacted by abuse. This is imperative as ministers and church leaders tend to be less educated compared to Baptist and Methodist clergy and administrators. The stories of the women in chapter 4 and the metrics in chapter 1 confirm the lack of education and awareness among pastors and the inability to adequately assist IPV victims. The church is in a prime position to augment awareness of the issue and develop effective strategies to combat abuse and provide a pathway for women to report. The church can position itself in the fight against abuse to be one of the leading faith-based entities that disseminates domestic violence education and awareness across the entire congregation and helps encourage women to report. The church must utilize the entire month of October as Domestic Violence Awareness Month to promote an awareness campaign that rivals breast cancer awareness.

Many congregations across the world have implemented a "breast cancer awareness Sunday" to highlight the issue, including early detection, treatment, and stories of survival. The success of this service has catapulted breast cancer awareness to a level almost unattainable by any other societal issue. The church should embrace Domestic Violence Awareness Month with the same vigor as breast cancer awareness. This could be inclusive of creating an ecumenical worship service to support victims and celebrate survivors of abuse. The next step is to move beyond the worship service and extend the campaign to include seminars, trainings, and educational sessions to increase awareness and equip parishioners with the tools to recognize the signs and symptoms of abuse and skills of how to assist victims.

The church must be encouraged to expand its community partnerships and encourage individuals to wear purple (the IPV awareness color) in the same manner as breast cancer awareness supporters wear pink. The church can be a powerful force in this campaign as many congregants are sports fans, entertainers, and business leaders in the community.

Followers of Christ should establish goals to measure the number of parishioners who receive training, ongoing education, and report possible incidents of abuse. The metrics captured will assist the church in reaching a significant number of congregants to augment awareness, analyze and revamp training, and understand trends of abuse to provide the most updated information on the issue. This is imperative for pastors and church leaders who have the propensity to spiritualize domestic violence in lieu of viewing the issue through the lens of victims. The church should embrace a collaborative holistic model and continue to build the fence of protection around victims and families. Christendom can ill afford to maintain a position of reaction to abuse, but must become increasingly proactive.

The notion of abuse has once again risen to the top of community issues and reignited the fight against IPV with the recent problems in the National Football League with players such as Jonathan Dwyer, Quincy Greg Hardy, Brandon Marshall, Ray McDonald, Ray Rice, as well as the Ultimate Fighting Championship fighters Thiago Silva and Anthony Johnson. The next step for disciples of Christ is to sustain the momentum of IPV awareness by developing year-long events and activities to keep the issue in the forefront with the hope of helping more women report. The Christian church must also be encouraged to assist victims in the healing process.

The healing process must be inclusive of individual counseling, marriage counseling (when appropriate), and family therapy, specifically for children impacted by domestic violence. The process can be a dual approach with spiritual disciplines and holistic therapy; however, the process cannot lean toward spirituality to the extent that counseling stands in the shadows of spirituality. Christendom has to be confident that healing can occur over time in safe spaces and will not always be immediate or miraculous. The church should also develop a program that helps abusive men who are willing to seek assistance and engage in ongoing counseling. There are limited programs specifically designed for men who abuse. The Christian church must view abuse through the lens of sin, serving these men with the goal of healing and reducing the number of occurrences. Ray Rice was recently reinstated back to the NFL as a result of the appeal process and many analysts are confident that he will play again, although some teams may be slow to offer Rice a contract. However, the issue moving forward is how the team that signs Rice will ensure that he receives ongoing counseling (along with his wife) to reduce the chances of domestic abuse reoccurring. The Black church in particular has perhaps the greatest opportunity to help men understand the nature of their issues and once again love their wives as they love themselves. Further, it is high time that the church become the prophetic voice to confront and challenge the oppression of the poor.

CONCLUSION

Oppression of the Poor

The instruction from the Lord in Exodus 22:21 prohibits Israel from oppressing or vexing strangers, as they themselves were strangers in the land of Egypt. Exodus 23:9 states the same instruction in 22:21.

Leviticus 25:14 warns Israel to cease from oppressing their neighbors. In Leviticus 25:17, the writer warns Israel not to oppress one another, but to fear God. In Deuteronomy 23:16, God states that servants should not be oppressed by their masters. Proverbs 14:31 states that the individual who oppresses the poor reproaches their creator, but those that honor God have mercy on the poor. The plight of the powerless and help for the poor (IPV victims) is the hope that God's people should offer women through the prophetic voice and leadership platform that the church has been granted by God to be the voice for the voiceless and strength for the powerless.

The church has the responsibility to strengthen victims that have been made feeble and offer hope—not only hope for the future, but hope for the present. The abuse victims that I interviewed understood that God was with them (although most acknowledged there were times when it did not feel like he was present); however, their foremost concern was the lack of understanding, education, and appropriate action by pastors and leaders and the feeling of hopelessness in addressing the issue through their lens. Those who identify as Jesus' disciples are encouraged to replicate his fight for the marginalized and challenge those in power, particularly male religious leaders who believe in the subjugation of women. The fight of Jesus for the marginalized must become the fight of the Black church and Christendom in the twenty-first century to bring hope for victims and families of IPV.

The future of IPV prevention in the Black church will be encouraged to provide more emphasis on services for men who abuse. There is a plethora of services and resources specifically focused on women and children, but lacking for abusers. The Black church must initiate a process to assist abusers that remain a part of the church. The church cannot spiritualize the intrinsic issues of abusers by simply stating that they are possessed by evil spirits in need of spiritual exorcism. Pastors and church leaders must address the problem head on and provide assistance to abusers as one of many methods to reduce the occurrences of IPV in the church.

The church will also have to address the problem of domestic violence among same-gender couples who attend worship services and are accepted as members in some denominations. Intimate partner violence is on the rise among same-sex couples, and as they become more involved in the life of the church, protocols must be in place to provide meaningful help to them as well.

Bibliography

Ahlstrom, Sydney E. *A Religious History of the American People*. 2nd ed. New Haven, CT: Yale University Press, 2004.
Alabama Coalition Against Domestic Violence. "Barriers to Leaving." http://www.acadv.org/barriers.html.
Amram. David Werner. *The Jewish Law of Divorce According to the Bible and Talmud*. New York: Hermon, 1986.
Arnold, Clinton E. *Ephesians: An Exegetical Commentary on the New Testament*. Grand Rapids: Zondervan, 2010.
Ashley, Timothy. *The Book of Numbers*. Grand Rapids: Eerdmans, 1993.
Bailey, Kenneth E. *Paul Through Mediterranean Eyes: Cultural Studies in 1 Corinthians*. Downers Grove, IL: InterVarsity, 2011.
Bancroft, Lundy. *Why Does He Do That?: Inside the Minds of Angry and Controlling Men*. New York: Berkley, 2002.
Barth, Markus. *Ephesians 4–6*. New Haven, CT: Yale University Press, 2008.
Battle, Michael. *The Black Church in America: African American Christian Spirituality*. Hoboken, NJ: Blackwell, 2006.
Belgrave, Faye Z., and Kevin W. Allison. *African American Psychology: From Africa to America*. Thousand Oaks, CA: Sage, 2010.
Belk, Judy. "On Sunday, Faith, and Freedom: Black Churches in the South Were Always About Much More than Religion." http://articles.latimes.com/2013/apr/07/opinion/la-oe-belk-religion-20130407.
Bergant, Diane. *Genesis: In the Beginning*. Collegeville, MN: Liturgical, 2013.
Berlin, Ira. *The Making of African America: The Four Great Migrations*. New York: Penguin, 2010.
Belt-Beyan, Phyllis M. *The Emergence of African American Literacy Traditions: Family and Community Efforts in the Nineteenth Century*. Westport, CT: Praeger, 2004.
Besharov, Douglas J. "Doing Something About Child Abuse: The Need to Narrow the Grounds for State Intervention." *Harvard J.L. & Pub. Pol'y* (1985) 539–90.
Best, Ernest. *Ephesians: A Exegetical and Critical Commentary*. New York: T. & T. Clark, 2004.
BlackDemographics.com. "The Black Church: African American Religious Affiliation." http://blackdemographics.com/culture/religion.

Bibliography

Black, Monika. "The Role of the Black Church in Addressing IPV at the Community Level." 2012. *College of Science and Health Theses and Dissertations*, Paper 22. http://via.library.depaul.edu/csh_etd/22.

Black, Robert, and Ronald McClung. *1 & 2 Timothy, Titus, and Philemon*. Indianapolis: Wesleyan, 2004.

Boice, James Montgomery. *Ephesians*. Grand Rapids: Baker, 2006.

Bowen, Ellen L. *Domestic Violence Treatment for Abusive Women: A Treatment Manual*. New York: Routledge, 2009.

Brant, Jo-Ann A. *John*. Grand Rapids: Baker Academic, 2011.

Brown, Raymond. *The Message of Numbers*. Downers Grove, IL: InterVarsity, 2002.

Browne, Angela. "Violence in Marriage: Until Death Do Us Part?" In *Violence Between Intimate Partners: Patterns, Causes, and Effects*, edited by Albert P. Cardarelli. Needham Heights, 54–55. MA: Allyn & Bacon, 1997.

Bureau of Crime and Research Statistics. "Crime & Socioeconomic Status." http://www.bocsar.nsw.gov.au/Pages/bocsar_topics/bocsar_pub_qtot_721934.aspx#socioeconomic.

Buzawa, Carl, Eve Buzawa, and Evan Stark. *Responding to Domestic Violence: The Integration of Criminal Justice and Human Services*. Thousand Oaks, CA: Sage, 2012.

Carmichael, Calum. *The Book of Numbers: A Critique of Genesis*. New Haven, CT: Yale University Press, 2012.

Carlson, Matthew J., Susan D. Harris, and George W. Holden. "Violence in the African American Family." *Journal of Family Violence* 14/2 (1999) 205–26.

Centers for Disease Control and Prevention. "Costs of Intimate Partner Violence against Women in the United States." Atlanta: CDC, National Center for Injury Prevention and Control, 2003. http://www.cdc.gov/ncipc/pub-res/ipv_cost/ipv.htm.

Chafe, William H., Raymond Gavins, and Robert Korstad. *Remembering Jim Crow: African Americans Tell About Life in the Segregated South*. New York: New Press, 2001.

Chase, David A., and David W. Holdren. *1–2 Peter, 1–3 John, and Jude*. Indianapolis: Wesleyan, 2006.

Child Welfare Information Gateway. "Clergy as Mandatory Reporters of Child Abuse and Neglect." Washington, DC: U.S. Department of Health and Human Services, Children's Bureau, 2014. https://www.childwelfare.gov/pubPDFs/clergymandated.pdf.

Clark, Ron. *Am I Sleeping with the Enemy?: Males and Females in the Image of God*. Eugene, OR: Cascade, 2010.

———. *The Better Way: The Church of Agape in Emerging Corinth*. Eugene, OR: Cascade, 2009.

———. "Family Management or Involvement: Paul's Use of *Prohistemi* 1 Timothy 3 as a Requirement for Church Leadership." *Stone Campbell Journal* (Fall 2006) 243.

———. *Freeing the Oppressed: A Call to Christians Concerning Domestic Abuse*. Eugene, OR: Cascade, 2009.

Collins, Raymond F. *I & II Timothy and Titus*. Louisville: Westminster John Knox, 2002.

Cone, James. *God of the Oppressed*. New York: Seabury, 1975.

Costen, Melva. *African American Worship*. Nashville: Abingdon, 1993.

Cracknell, Kenneth, and Susan J. White. *Introduction to World Methodism*. New York: Cambridge University Press, 2005.

Deterding, Paul E. *Colossians*. St. Louis: Concordia, 2003.

Bibliography

Dixon, Patricia. *African American Relationships, Marriages, and Families: An Introduction.* New York: Routledge, 2007.

Domestic Abuse Intervention Programs. "Wheel Gallery." http://www.theduluthmodel.org/training/wheels.html.

DuPage County. "Model Policy: Reporting Child Abuse and Neglect for School Officials in DuPage County." https://www.dupageroe.org/wp-content/uploads/Mandated_Reporting.pdf.

Dugan, Meg Kennedy, and Roger R. Hock. *It's My Life Now: Starting Over After an Abusive Relationship or Domestic Violence.* New York: Routledge, 2006.

Durose, Matthew R., et al. "Family Violence Statistics: Including Statistics on Strangers and Acquaintances." U.S. Department of Justice, NCJ 207846. 2005. http://www.bjs.gov/content/pub/pdf/fvs.pdf.

Dutton, Donald, and Susan K. Golant. *The Batterer: A Psychological Profile.* New York: Basic Books, 1995.

Dvorak, Katharine. *An African American Exodus: The Segregation of the Southern Churches.* Brooklyn: Carlson, 1991.

Evans, Christopher H. *Histories of American Christianity: An Introduction.* Waco, TX: Baylor University Press, 2013.

Evans, Craig A. *Matthew.* New York: Cambridge University Press, 2012.

Evans, Patricia. *The Verbally Abusive Relationship: How to Recognize It and How to Respond.* Avon, MA: Adam Media, 2010.

Finkelhor, David, Lisa Jones, and Anne Shuttuch. "Updated Trends in Child Maltreatment." University of New Hampshire, Crimes Against Children Research Center, 2010.

Fiore, Benjamin. *The Pastoral Epistles: First Timothy, Second Timothy, Titus.* Edited by Daniel J. Harrington. Collegeville, MN: Liturgical, 2007.

Foster, Frances Smith. *'Til Death or Distance Do Us Part: Love and Marriage in African America.* New York: Oxford University Press, 2009.

Foulkes, Francis. *Ephesians.* Downers Grove, IL: IPV Academic, 2007.

Fowl, Stephen E. *Ephesians: A Commentary.* Louisville: Westminster John Knox, 2012.

Fox, Michael V. *Proverbs 10-31.* New Haven, CT: Yale University Press, 2009.

Franklin, John Hope. "African American Families: A Historical Note." In *Black Families*, edited by Harriette Pipes McAdoo, 5-9. 3rd ed. Thousand Oaks, CA: Sage, 1997.

Frederick, Marla F. *Between Sundays: Black Women and Everyday Struggles of Faith.* Los Angeles: University of California Press, 2003.

Garcia, Vanessa, and Patrick McManimon. *Gendered Justice: Intimate Partner Violence and the Criminal Justice System.* Boulder, CO: Rowan & Littlefield, 2011.

Garland, David E. *1 Corinthians.* Grand Rapids: Baker Academic, 2003.

Gelles, Richard J. *Intimate Violence in Families.* 3rd ed. Thousand Oaks, CA: Sage, 1997.

Gilkes, Cheryl Townsend. *If It Wasn't for the Woman: Black Women's Experience and Womanist Culture in Church and Community.* New York: Orbis, 2001.

Goldingay, John. *Numbers and Deuteronomy for Everyone.* Louisville: Westminster John Knox, 2010.

Green Ricky K. *Voices in Black Political Thought.* New York: Peter Lang, 2005.

Grudem, Wayne. *1 Peter.* Downers Grove, IL: IVP Academic, 2007.

Gupta, Nijay K. *Colossians.* Macon, GA: Smyth & Helwys, 2013.

Guthrie, Donald. *The Pastoral Epistles.* Downers Grove, IL: InterVarsity, 2007.

Haley, Shawn, and Ellie Braun Haley. *War on the Home Front: An Examination of Wife Abuse.* New York: Berghahn, 2000.

Bibliography

Hammond, Geordan. "John Wesley's Relations with the Lutheran Pietist Clergy in Georgia." In *The Pietist Impulse in Christianity*, edited by Christopher T. Collins Winn, 135–45.Eugene, OR: Pickwick, 2011.

Hampton, R. L. Hampton, and R. J. Gelles. "Violence toward Black Women in a Nationally Representative Sample of Black Families." *Journal of Comparative Family Studies* 25/1 (1994) 105–19.

Hampton, Robert, William Oliver, and Lucia Magarian. "Domestic Violence in the African American Community: An Analysis of Social and Structural Factors." *Violence Against Women* 9/5 (2003) 533–57.

Harris, John Glyndwr. *Christian Theology: The Spiritual Tradition*. Portland, OR: Sussex Academic, 2001.

Harvard Black Law Students Association. "Domestic Violence—Sad Facts." http://blogs.law.harvard.edu/hblsasj/2009/10/31/domestic-violence-sad-facts.

Harvey, E. L. "The Price of Discipleship." In *Portraits of a Generation: Early Pentecostal Leaders*, edited by James R. Goff Jr. and Grant Wacker, 30–32. Fayetteville: University of Arkansas Press, 2002.

Harvey, Paul. "'That Was about Equalization after Freedom': Southern Evangelism and the Politics of Reconstruction and Redemption, 1861–1900." In *Vale of Tears: New Essays on Religion and Reconstruction*, edited by Edward J Blum and W. Scott Pool, 73–92. Macon GA: Mercer University Press, 2005.

Hassouneh-Phillips, Dena. "Strength and Vulnerability: Spirituality in Abused American Muslim Women's Lives." *Issues in Mental Health Nursing* 24/6–7 (2003) 681–94.

Hempton, David. *Methodism: Empire of the Spirit*. New Haven, CT: Yale University Press, 2005.

Hendriksen, William, and Simon J. Kistemaker. *Thessalonians, the Pastorals, and Hebrews*. Grand Rapids: Baker, 2004.

Hill, Samuel S. *One Name but Several Faces: Variety in Popular Christian Denominations in Southern History*. Athens: University of Georgia Press, 1996.

Hill, Sheryl A. *Black Intimacies: A Gender Perspective on Families and Relationships*. New York: Altamira, 2005.

Hoehner, Harold W. *Ephesians: An Exegetical Commentary*. Grand Rapids: Baker Academic, 2002.

Hoff, Bert H. "CDC Study: More Men than Women Victims of Partner Abuse." Stop Abusive and Violent Environments. http://www.saveservices.org/2012/02/cdc-study-more-men-than-women-victims-of-partner-abuse.

Hooks, Bell. *We Real Cool: Black Men & Masculinity*. New York: Routledge, 2004.

Hopkins, Dwight N. *Down, Up, and Over: Slave Religion and Black Theology*. Minneapolis: Fortress, 2000.

Horne, Milton P. *Proverbs–Ecclesiastes*. Macon, GA: Smyth & Helwys, 2003.

Jefferson College of Health Sciences. "Cycle of Abuse in Relationships." http://www.jchs.edu/jchs-voice-program-cycle-abuse-and-power-control-wheel.

Johnson, Alan F. *1 Corinthians*. Downers Grove, IL: IVP Academic, 2004.

Johnson, Leanor, Boulin Johnson, and Robert Staples. *Black Families at the Crossroads: Challenges and Prospects*. San Francisco: Jossey-Bass, 2005.

Johnson, Paul E. *African American Christianity: Essay in History*. Los Angeles: University of California Press, 1994.

Bibliography

Joyner, Charles. "'Believer I Know': The Emergence of African-American Christianity." In *African-American Christianity: Essays in History*, edited by Paul E. Johnson, 20–36. Berkeley: University of California Press, 1994.

Kaslow, Nadine, Sheridan Thorn, and Anuradha Paranjpe. "Interventions for Abused African American Women and Their Children." In *Interpersonal Violence in the African American Community: Evidence-Based Prevention and Treatment Practices*, edited by Robert Hampton and Thomas Gullotta, 47–80. New York: Springer, 2006.

Kistemaker, Simon. *1 Corinthians: New Testament Commentary*. Grand Rapids, MI: Baker Books, 2004.

Keener, Craig S. *1–2 Corinthians*. New York: Cambridge University Press, 2005.

Kempe, Henry C., and Ray E. Helfer, editors. *The Battered Child*. Chicago: Chicago University Press, 1968.

Keyssar, Alexander. *The Right to Vote: The Contested History of Democracy in the United States*. New York: Basic, 2009.

Knapton, Sarah. "Educated and Well Paid Women More Likely to Suffer Domestic Abuse." *The Telegraph*, March 6, 2014. http://www.telegraph.co.uk/journalists/sarah-knapton/10679238/Educated-and-well-paid-women-more-likely-to-suffer-domestic-abuse.html.

Kovacs, Judith L. *1 Corinthians: Interpreted by Early Christian Commentators*. Edited by Robert Louis Wilken. Grand Rapids: Eerdmans, 2005.

Krason, Stephen. "The Critics of Current Child Abuse Laws and the Child Protective System: A Survey of the Leading Literature." *Catholic Social Science Review* 12 (2007) 307–50.

Krause, Deborah. *1 Timothy*. New York: T. & T. Clark, 2004.

La Sor, William Sanford, David Allan Hubbard, and Frederic William Bush. *Old Testament Survey: The Message, Form, and Background of the Old Testament*. 2nd ed. Grand Rapids: Eerdmans, 1996.

Lawson, Tony, and Joan Garrod. *Dictionary of Sociology*. Chicago: Fitzroy Dearborn, 2001.

Leonard, Bill J. *Baptists in America*. New York: Columbia University Press, 2005.

National Park Service. "First African Baptist Church." *Lexington, Kentucky: The Athens of the West*. http://www.nps.gov/nr/travel/lexington/fab.htm.

Liefield, Walter L. *Ephesians*. Downers Grove, IL: InterVarsity, 1997.

Lincoln, C. Eric. *The Black Church in the African American Experience*. Durham, NC: Duke University Press, 1990.

Lockwood, Gregory J. *1 Corinthians*. St. Louis: Concordia, 2010.

Long, D. Stephen. *Hebrews: A Theological Commentary on the Bible*. Louisville: Westminster John Knox, 2011.

Longman, Tremper, III. *Proverbs*. Grand Rapids: Baker Academic, 2004.

Lummis, Artis T. "'Heart and Head' in Reaching Pastors of Black Churches." 2006. Hartford Institute for Religion Research. http://hirr.hartsem.edu/bookshelf/lummis_article5.html.

Macartney, Suzanne, Alemayehu Bishaw, and Kayla Fontenot. "American Community Survey Briefs". ACSBR/11-11. Issued February 2013.

Matthews, Ben, and Maureen C. Kenny. "Mandatory Reporting Legislation in the United States, Canada, and Australia: A Cross-Jurisdictional Review of Key Features, Differences, and Issues." *Child Maltreatment* 13/1 (2008) 50–63.

Martin, Elmer P., and Joanne Mitchell Martin. *Spirituality and the Black Helping Tradition in Social Work*. Washington, DC: National Association of Social Workers, 2002.

Bibliography

Martinson, Lisa M. "An Analysis of Racism and Resources for African-American Female Victims of Domestic Violence in Wisconsin." *Wisconsin Women's Law Journal* 16 (2001) 259–85.

Maxwell, John. *Developing the Leader within You*. Nashville: T. Nelson, 1993.

McAdoo, Harriette Pipes, and John L. McAdoo. *The Dynamics of African American Fathers' Family Roles*. Michigan Family Review 3/1 (1997) 7–15. http://hdl.handle.net/2027/spo.4919087.0003.102.

McAdoo, John L. "The Roles of African American Fathers in the Socialization of Their Children." In *Black Families*, edited by Harriette Pipes McAdoo, 3–9. 3rd ed. Thousand Oaks, CA: Sage, 1997.

McCarren, Paul J. *Matthew: A Simple Guide*. New York: Rowman & Littlefiled, 2012.

McKane, William. *Proverbs*. OTL. London: SCM, 1970.

McKeown, James. *Genesis*. Grand Rapids: Eerdmans, 2008.

McCue, Margi Laird. *Domestic Violence: A Reference Handbook*. Santa Barbara, ACA: ABC-CLIO, 1995.

———. *Domestic Violence: A Reference Handbook*. 2nd ed. Santa Barbara, CA: ABC-CLIO, 2008.

Melton, J. Gordon. *A Will to Choose: The Origins of African American Methodism*. Lanham, MD: Rowan & Littlefield, 2007.

Miles, Al. *Domestic Violence: What Every Pastor Needs to Know*. Minneapolis: Fortress, 2000.

———. *Ending Violence in Teen Dating Relationships: A Resource Guide for Parents and Pastors*. Minneapolis: Augsburg, 2005.

Milgrom, Jacob. *Leviticus*. Minneapolis: Fortress, 2004.

Moore, Thorn. "The African-American Church: A Source of Empowerment, Mutual Help, and Social Change." *Journal of Prevention and Intervention in the Community* 10/1 (1991) 147–67.

Morris, Leon Morris. *1 Corinthians*. Downers Grove, IL: InterVarsity, 2007.

Muddiman, John. *The Epistle to the Ephesians*. New York: Hendrickson, 2004.

Mullen, Paul E., Michele Pathé, and Rosemary Purcell. *Stalkers and Their Victims*. 2nd ed. New York: Cambridge University Press, 2009.

Nash, Robert Scott. *1 Corinthians*. Macon, GA: Smyth & Helwys, 2009.

National Center for Prosecution of Child Abuse. "Mandatory Reporting of Child Abuse and Neglect." 2012. http://www.ndaa.org/pdf/Mandatory%20Reporting%20of%20Child%20Abuse%20and%20Neglect-nov2012.pdf.

National Poverty Center. "Poverty in the United States Frequently Asked Questions." University of Michigan Gerald R. Ford School of Public Policy. http://www.npc.umich.edu/poverty/.

National Resource Center on Domestic Violence. "DVAM Events." http://www.nrcdv.org/dvam/DVAM-Events.

Nowell, Irene. *Numbers*. Collegeville, MN: Liturgical, 2011.

O'Brien, Peter T. *The Letter to the Ephesians*. Grand Rapids: Eerdmans, 1999.

Oregon Department of Human Services. "Child Abuse and Neglect Reporting Numbers." http://www.oregon.gov/dhs/children/pages/abuse/cps/report.aspx.

———. "Mandatory Reporting." http://www.oregon.gov/dhs/abuse/pages/mandatory_report.aspx.

Oster, Rick. *1 Corinthians*. Joplin, MO: College Press, 1995.

Pao, David W. *Colossians & Philemon*. Grand Rapids: Zondervan, 2012.

Bibliography

Pew Research Center. "A Religious Portrait of African Americans." January 30, 2009. http://www.pewforum.org/2009/01/30/a-religious-portrait-of-african-americans.

Phillips, John. *Exploring 1 Corinthians: An Expository Commentary*. Grand Rapids: Kregel, 2002.

Placher, William C. *The Domestication of Transcendence: How Modern Thinking About God Went Wrong*. Louisville: Westminster John Knox, 1996.

Podles, Leon. *The Church Impotent: The Feminization of Christianity*. Dallas: Spence, 1999.

Pratt, Richard L. *I & II Corinthians*. Nashville: Broadman & Holman, 2000.

The Rave Project. "Looking at the Data . . . from Church Women." http://www.theraveproject.com/index.php/resources/resource/looking_at_the_data_from_church_women.

Rennison, Callie Marie. "Intimate Partner Violence, 1993–2001." U.S. Department of Justice, Bureau of Justice Statistics, Crime Data Brief. NCJ 197838. November 2003. http://www.bjs.gov/content/pub/pdf/ipv.pdf.

Rennison, Callie Marie, and Sarah Welchans. "Intimate Partner Violence." U.S. Department of Justice, Bureau of Justice Statistics, Crime Data Brief. NCJ 178247. May 2000. http://www.bjs.gov/content/pub/ascii/ipv.txt.

Riches, John. *Galatians Through the Centuries*. Malden, MA: Blackwell, 2008.

Robinson, Anthony B., and Robert W. Wall. *Called to Lead: Paul's Letter to Timothy for a New Day*. Grand Rapids: Eerdmans, 2012.

Robinson, Cedric J. *Black Movements in America*. New York: Routledge, 1997.

Sanders, Susan M. *Teen Dating Violence: The Invisible Peril*. New York: Peter Lang, 2003.

Scafidi, Susan. *Who Owns Culture?: Appropriation and Authenticity in American Law*. Piscataway, NJ: Rutgers University Press, 2005.

Schenck, Kenneth. *1 & 2 Corinthians: A Commentary for Bible Students*. Indianapolis: Wesleyan, 2006.

Schewe, Paul A., ed. *Preventing Violence in Relationships: Interventions Across the Life Span*. Washington, DC: American Psychological Association, 2002.

Schuetze, Armin W. *1 Timothy, 2 Timothy, Titus*. St. Louis: Concordia, 1993.

Shipway, Lyn. *Domestic Violence: A Handbook for Health Professionals*. New York: Routledge, 2004.

Shouse, Aimee D. *Women's Rights: Documents Decoded*. Santa Barbara, CA: BC-CLIO, 2014.

Stalking Resource Center. "Stalking Information." http://www.victimsofcrime.org/our-programs/stalking-resource-center/stalking-information.

Stanford, Anthony. *Homophobia in the Black Church: How Faith, Politics, and Fear Divide the Black Community*. Santa Barbara, CA: ABL-CLIO, 2013.

Stott, John R. W. *The Message of 1 Timothy & Titus*. Downers Grove, IL: InterVarsity, 2001.

Strong, Douglas M. "American Methodism in the Nineteenth Century: Expansion and Fragmentation." In *The Cambridge Companion to American Methodism*, edited by Jason E. Vickers, 63–72. New York: Cambridge University Press, 2013.

Stubbs, David. *Numbers*. Grand Rapids: Brazos, 2009.

Talbert, Charles H. *Matthew*. Grand Rapids: Baker Academic, 2010.

Tamez, Elsa. *Early Christianity: A Study of the First Letter to Timothy*. New York: Orbis, 2007.

Taylor, Robert Joseph, Linda M. Chatters, and Jeff Levin. *Religion in the Lives of African Americans: Social, Psychological, and Health Perspectives*. Thousand Oaks, CA: Sage, 2004.

Bibliography

Thielman, Frank. *Ephesians*. Grand Rapids: Baker Academic, 2010.

Thompson, M.P. & Others. "Partner Violence, Social Support, and Distress among Inner-City African American Women." *American Journal of Community Psychology* 28 (2000) 127–32.

Todd, Margo. "A People's Reformation?" In *Reformation Christianity*, edited by Peter Matheson, 70–95. People's History of Christianity 5. Minneapolis: Fortress, 2007.

Toppe, Carleton A. *First Corinthians*. People's Bible Commentary. St. Louis: Concordia, 2005.

Tucker, M. Belinda, and Angela D. James. "New Families, New Functions: Postmodern African American Families in Context." In *African American Family Life: Ecological and Cultural Diversity*, edited by Vonnie C. McLoyd, Nancy E. Hill, and Kenneth A. Dodge, 94–95. New York: Guilford, 2005.

Towner, Philip H. *The Letters to Timothy and Titus*. Grand Rapids: Eerdmans, 2006.

Tjaden, Patricia, and Nancy Thoennes. "Extent, Nature, and Consequences of Intimate Partner Violence: Findings From the National Violence Against Women Survey." U.S. Department of Justice Office of Justice Programs and the National Institute of Justice. NCJ 181867. July 2000. https://www.ncjrs.gov/pdffiles1/nij/181867.pdf.

Verdal, Juliet. "Broken Silence: Polls Show Lack of Conversation on Domestic, Sexual Violence in Churches." Sojourners, June 19, 2014. http://sojo.net/blogs/2014/06/19/broken-silence-poll-shows-lack-conversation-domestic-sexual-violence-churches.

Violence Policy Center. "When Men Murder Women: An Analysis of 2002 Homicide Data: Females Murdered by Males in Single Victim/Single Offender Incidents." September 2004. http://www.vpc.org/studies/wmmw2004.pdf.

Walker, Lenore. *The Battered Woman Syndrome*. New York: Springer, 1984.

———. *The Battered Woman Syndrome*. 2nd ed. New York: Springer, 2000.

Wallace, Beverly. *A Womanist Legacy of Trauma, Grief, and Loss: Reframing the Notion of the Strong Black Woman*. Minneapolis: Fortress, 2010.

Whelcher, L. H. *The History and Heritage of African American Churches: A Way Out of No Way*. St. Paul, MN: Paragon, 2011.

Whitford, David. *Luther: A Guide for the Perplexed*. New York: T. & T. Clark, 2011.

Williamson, Peter. *Ephesians*. Grand Rapids: Baker, 2009.

Winter, Bruce W. *After Paul Left Corinth: The Influence of Secular Ethics and Social Change*. Grand Rapids: Eerdmans, 2001.

Woodley, Matt. *The Gospel of Matthew: God with Us*. Downers Grove, IL: InterVarsity, 2011.

Wright, N. T. *1 Corinthians*. Paul for Everyone. Louisville: Westminster John Knox, 2004.

———. *The Pastoral Letters: 1 and 2 Timothy and Titus*. Paul for Everyone. Louisville: Westminster John Knox, 2004.

———. *Colossians and Philemon*. Tyndale New Testament Commentaries 12. Downers Grove, IL: IVP Academic, 2007.

Index

abuse. *See* cycle of abuse; domestic violence; Power and Control Wheel
abusers
   accountability to, 96
   controlling behavior of, 9
   counseling for, 116–17
   intimidation behaviors, 13–14
   methodology of, 1
   personality of, 2
   signs and symptoms of, 8–9. *See also* control/controlling behavior
   stalkers vs., 7
acting out phase of abuse cycle, 11
active listening, 84
acute explosion phase of abuse cycle, 11
agape, 67
Allen, Richard, 25
AME church, 25
anxiety, 8–9, 18, 71, 83
Asian women, 16
authentein, 64
avoidance, as sign of IPV, 8
Azusa Street Revival, 4, 22, 25, 27–28, 43

Bjelland, Heidi Fischer, 15–16
Black Americans, 4. *See also* Black males; Black women

Black church
   bylaws embedding IPV policy, 110–12
   as center of Black community, 96
   church mother, 38–39
   in Civil Rights era, 27–29
   community collaboration, 111–13
   community culture, 29–30
   denominations of, 23, 25
   domestic violence in, 18–21
   factors enabling violence in, 19–20
   female roles in, 37–39
   history of, 24–25
   ideology of community and, 20
   institutionalizing IPV awareness, 111
   internal IPV policy development, 106–10
   in Jim Crow era, 26–27
   launching pad for, 25
   leadership positions in, 36–37
   oldest known, 26
   pastoral care departments, 106–10
   as place of empowerment, 96
   rise of, 27–28
   role of wives in, 65
   theological mandate for reporting abuse, 101–2
   worship styles, 26–27

Index

Black males. *See also* husbands
   in church environment, 34–37
   as head of household, 32
   as leader of family, 33–34
   as pastor, 35–37
   as patriarch, 31
   as protector, 34
   as provider, 32–33
Black theology. *See also* New Testament; Old Testament
   holiness movement, 43
   male leadership, 43
   origins of, 43
Black women. *See also* White women; wives
   brawling, 50–51
   church role of, 37–39
   codependent on men, 53
   comparing to continual dripping, 50
   for creation and enlightenment of man, 64
   domestic duties of, 37, 38
   education level of, 38
   family role of, 37
   IPV rates of, 6–7, 16
   keeping silent, 63
   Lady Wisdom, 52–53
   learning in same manner as men, 64–65
   no authority in the church, 63–64
   as second-class citizens, 50
   submission to men, 37, 61
   subordinate to men, 58
   who preach, 64–65
   worthy, 52
blaming, action of, 89
Boice, James, 67

calm phase of abuse cycle, 12
Carmichael, Calum, 48
Centers for Disease Control (CDC), 6
Child Abuse Act (Oregon), 99
Child Abuse Prevention and Treatment Act (CAPTA), 98
children
   anxiety experienced by, 18
   impact of IPV on, 18, 79–80
   post-traumatic stress disorder (PTSD) in, 18
Christian Methodist Episcopal Church (CME), 25
church mother, 38–39
Civil Rights Movement, 22, 27–29
Clark, Ron, 39, 55
clergy-penitent confidentiality, 100
Colored Methodist Episcopal Church, 25
Colossians, 61–62
community collaboration, 111–13, 115
Cone, James, 43
confidants, survivor, 83–86, 88
control/controlling behavior
   gifts for silence, 74
   inside/outside of house, 73–74
   over finances, 74
   Power and Control Wheel, 12–14, 13
   as sign of IPV, 9
   stalking and, 7–8
Corinthians, 57–61
culture
   of Black Church, 29–31
   of community, 29–30
   of congregation, 30
   defined gender roles, 31
   definition of, 29
   embedding IPV in church, 102
cycle of abuse, 9–12, 10, 91. *See also* Power and Control Wheel

date murderers, 5
depression, 79
Deuteronomy, 117
Devery, Christopher, 15
divorce, 54–55
domestic abuse, 1
domestic violence. *See also* intimate partner violence; survivor advice; survivors; violence
   in black church, 18–21
   blaming wife to justify husband's behavior, 89
   congregation impact of, 81–83
   definition of, 1

Index

early signs and symptoms, 91
family impact of, 79–80
impact of, 78–79
media attention on, 4
pastor's voice and influence to change, 40
prayer and fasting to resolve, 88
rates of, 5–6
resources and services, 113. *See also* IPV prevention
risk factors, 14–18
of same-gender couples, 117–18
socioeconomic status and, 15
spirituality and, 19
survivor impact, 78–79
survivors of. *See* survivors
victims of. *See* victims
Domestic Violence Awareness Month, 102, 115
DuPage County School District, 100
Durret, Peter, 26

education
advocate level of, 104–5
Blacks denied, 44–45
developing training materials, 102
on domestic violence, 41
experienced level of, 104
importance of, 85
intermediate level of, 104
introductory level of, 103–4
on signs and symptoms of abuse, 92
women learning in same manner as men, 64–65
educational campaign, 103–5
Ephesians, 65–68
episcope, 62
Evers, Medgar, 28
external shame, 76–77

faith, misguided, 87–88
fear
awareness of, 91
to control and abuse, 72–73
of losing children, 73, 75
of reporting, 114. *See also* reporting abuse
of retaliation, 75
as sign of IPV, 8
femininity, 24, 39, 93
fence approach, 112–13
First African Church, 26
Foulkes, Francis, 66

Genesis narrative, 46–47
gifts for silence, 74
Gnostics, 64
Great Awakening, 26
The Gullahs, 30

haustefal codes, 56–57, 69
head of household, 32, 57, 62–63
Hispanic women, 16
Hoehner, Harold W., 66
holiness movement, 43
homicide, 7
hood, 60
house codes, 56–57, 69
husbands. *See also* Black males
as head of household, 62–63
to honor and praise wives, 62
love demonstrated for wife, 67
responsibility for marriage, 66
sanctifying and cleansing wives, 68
wives submitting to, 66–67

internal policy development, 106–10
internal shame, 77
interpersonal violence, 2
intimacy, 58
intimate partner violence. *See also* domestic violence; IPV prevention
behaviors of, 1
men as victims of, 6
rates of, 5–6
signs and symptoms of, 8–9
intimidation, behaviors of, 13–14
IPV prevention
assisting abusers, 117
awareness campaigns, 102
bylaws embedding IPV policy, 110–12
community collaboration, 111–13

Index

IPV prevention (*continued*)
    educational campaign, 103–5
    encouraging women to report, 96
    fence approach, 112–13
    future of, 117
    mandatory reporters, 98–101
    theological mandate for reporting abuse, 101–2
    training and educating pastors, 96

Jefferson College of Health Sciences (JCHS), 11
Jim Crow era, 23–24, 26–30, 34, 44, 96

Kempe, Henry, 98
King, Martin Luther, Jr., 28
Knapton, Sarah, 15

Lady Wisdom, 52–53
law enforcement, 76
leadership, 33–34, 40, 43
Leviticus, 101, 117
literacy and writing issues, 44–45

male dominance
    Civil Rights Movement and, 29
    cultural tradition of White, 28
    Paul on, 66
    pre-fall philosophy and, 57
    preserving through Scripture, 63
    theological foundation of, 30, 43, 50
mandatory reporters, 98–101
marriage. *See also* husbands; wives
    abstaining from intimacy, 58
    in Black culture, 39–40
    church encouraging mutual dependence in, 60
    before the fall, 46
    God's intent regarding, 55–56
    New Testament philosophy, 55
    post-fall understanding of, 55–56
    pre-fall philosophy, 55, 69
    roles and responsibilities in, 57–61, 66, 68, 93
    theology of, 46–47
masculinity, 39
McKane, William, 51

McKeown, James, 47
megachurches, 23
men
    as hypersexual initiators of sex, 58
    negative behavior of, 51
    selecting mates for daughters, 48–49
    as victims of IPV, 6
    women codependent on, 53
mental anguish, 72
Meredith, James, 28
Methodist movement, 25
Miles, Al, 3
Miles, William, 25
Morris, Leon, 59

National Association for the Advancement of Colored People (NAACP), 27
National Baptist Association, 25
National Center for Law and Economic Justice, 16
National Intimate Partner and Sexual Violence Survey (NISVS), 6
National Poverty Center (NPC), 16
National Violence Against Women Survey (NVAWS), 6
New Testament
    on cleansing, 68
    Colossians, 61–62
    Corinthians, 57–61
    on divorce, 54–55
    Ephesians, 65–68
    episcope, 62
    on head of household, 57
    husbands honoring and praising wives, 62
    on marriage, 55–56
    Matthew and Mark, 54–56
    pastors having own house in order, 62–63
    Paul, 55–56
    Timothy, 62–63
    wives subjecting to husbands, 61–62
    women for creation and enlightenment of man, 64
    women to keep silent, 63
Numbers, 47–49

Index

Obama, Barack, 4
Old Testament
  brawling women, 50–51
  Genesis narrative, 46–47
  God's patience with Israel, 47–48
  men selecting mates for daughters, 48–49
  Numbers, 47–49
  presence of God among his people, 47
  Proverbs, 49–53
  women as second-class citizens, 50
oppression, 28, 30, 48, 51, 117–18
Oregon, state of
  Child Abuse Act, 99
  human resources department, 106–7
  mandatory reporting, 99–100
  Temporary Assistance for Domestic Violence Survivors (TA-DVS), 107–8
  Temporary Assistance for Needy Families (TANF) program, 107
Oster, Rick, 60
Oxygen Network, 22

pastoral care departments, 106–10
pastors
  Black families trust in, 35
  Black males as, 35–37
  changing course of domestic violence, 40
  clergy-penitent confidentiality, 100
  congregation spiritual direction and formation by, 36
  having own house in order, 62–63
  income, 23
  IPV training for, 96
  literacy and writing issues of, 44–45
  as mandatory reporters, 100–101
  speaking about sexual abuse, 3
  understanding theological impact of not addressing IPV, 69
Paul, Saint, 55–56, 57–59
Pentecostal faith-based community, 22
Peter, Saint, 61–62

Pew Research for Religion and Public Life Project, 3–4
Pharisees, 54–55
Pietistic movement, 25
Podles, Leon, 39
policy development, 105
post-traumatic stress disorder (PTSD), 18
poverty rates, 16
Power and Control Wheel, 13, 48–50, 91. *See also* cycle of abuse
power structure
  to enslave Blacks, 27
  fighting against, 28
  genesis of male leadership and, 24–25
  post-fall understanding of, 53–54
  stalking and, 7–8
  unevenly allocated in relationship, 15
  against women, 48, 49–50
Preachers of L.A. (television show), 22
prohistemi, 63
Proverbs, 49–53

race/ethnicity, 16
racial segregation, 26
Randolph, Asa Phillip, 28
reconciliation phase of abuse cycle, 12
Religion and Violence e-Learning Project (RAVE), 2
reporting abuse
  fear of, 75–76, 114
  law enforcement and, 76
  mandatory laws, 98
  mandatory reporters, 98–101
  models of, 98–99
  protocol in Black church for, 97–102
  rate of occurrences before, 94
  shame in, 76–78
  in state of Oregon, 99–100
  women's hesitance to, 97
Rice, Ray, 4, 116
risk factors, 14–18
Rustin, Bayard, 28

Index

same-sex couples, 117–18
scripture. *See* New Testament; Old Testament; theology
self-confidence, lack of, 77–78
Seymour, William, 25
shame, 76–78
signs and symptoms of intimate partner violence, 8–9, 90, 91
socioeconomic status, 15–17
Southern Christian Leadership Conference (SCLC), 27
spirituality
    domestic violence and, 19
    misguided faith, 87–88
    violence veiled under guise of, 36
spouse murderers, 5
stalking, 7–8
Steele, Brandt, 98
Suffrage Movement, 27
suicide, 73, 79
survivor advice
    be aware of fear, 91
    becoming a better wife, 89
    education about abuse, 92
    prayer and fasting, 88
    prevention practice, 91–92
    recognize warning signs, 90
    recommendations on treating husband, 90
    spirituality as answer, 87–88
survivors. *See also* survivor advice; victims
    congregation impact of, 81–83
    correct interpretation of Scripture, 93
    early signs and symptoms, 91
    education, importance of, 85
    emotional support for, 83–84
    escape plans, 83–84
    family impact of, 79–80
    fear. *See* fear
    feeling validated, 85–87
    impact on, 78–79
    mental anguish of, 72
    offering misguided faith to, 87–88
    self-confidence, lack of, 77–78
    shame and, 76–78

temporary assistance for, 107–8
trust factor, 83

Temporary Assistance for Domestic Violence Survivors (TA-DVS), 107
Temporary Assistance for Needy Families (TANF) program, 107–8
tension-building phase of abuse cycle, 11
theological foundations of Black Church. *See* Black Theology
theology. *See also* New Testament; Old Testament
    definition of, 42
    Genesis narrative, 46–47
    of marriage, 46–47
Timothy, 62–63
transparency, 82
trust, 83

Urban League, 27
U.S. Census Bureau, 15, 16
U.S. Religious Landscape Survey, 3

Vanderhost, Richard H., 25
victims. *See also* survivors
    healing process, 116
    men as, 6
    perception of, 1
    of stalking, 7
violence. *See also* domestic violence
    in black church. *See* Black Church
    factors enabling, 19–20
    interpersonal, 2
    survivors of. *See* survivors
    veiled under guise of spirituality, 36
    victims of. *See* victims
vow, definition of, 48

Walker, Lenore, 10
warning signs, recognizing, 90
Wesley, Charles, 25
Wesley, John, 25
White slave masters, 26, 33, 96
White women, 6–7, 16–17. *See also* wives

Index

Whitefield, George, 25
Williams, Michael, 19
Winter, Bruce, 60
wives. *See also* Black women
   accepting blame, 89
   glorious and radiant, 68
   honoring cultural traditions, 19
   husbands honoring and praising, 62
   husbands sanctifying and cleansing, 68
   protecting husbands, 19
   receiving blame for husband's behavior, 89
   role in Black church, 65
   in subjection to husbands, 61–62
   submitting to husbands, 66–67
   as subordinate to husbands, 19
women in the church
   IPV and, 2–3
   key leadership roles of, 36–37
Women's Suffrage Movement, 27
Wright, N. T., 64

Young, Whitney, 28